50
American Serial Killers You've Probably Never Heard Of

Volume One

Robert Keller

Please Leave Your Review of This Book At http://bit.ly/kellerbooks

ISBN-13 978-1535138314

ISBN-10: 1535138319

© 2016 by Robert Keller

robertkellerauthor.com

All rights reserved.

No part of this publication may be copied or reproduced in any format, electronic or otherwise, without the prior, written consent of the copyright holder and publisher. This book is for informational and entertainment purposes only and the author and publisher will not be held responsible for the misuse of information contain herein, whether deliberate or incidental.

Much research, from a variety of sources, has gone into the compilation of this material. To the best knowledge of the author and publisher, the material contained herein is factually correct. Neither the publisher, nor author will be held responsible for any inaccuracies.

Table of Contents

50 American Serial Killers 7
Howard Arthur Allen 9
Amy Archer-Gilligan 12
Benjamin Atkins 15
Jake Bird 18
Dallen Bounds 22
Judy Buenoano 25
Dean Philip Carter 29
Joseph Christopher 32
Juan Covington 36
Andre Crawford 40
Brian Dugan 43
Edward Wayne Edwards 46
Donald Leroy Evans 50
Joseph Paul Franklin 53
Janie Lou Gibbs 56
Bertha Gifford 59
Kristen Gilbert 62
Billy Glaze 65
Billy Gohl 68
David Alan Gore 71

Dana Sue Gray 75

James Waybern Hall 79

Charles Ray Hatcher 82

Dale Hausner 86

J. Frank Hickey 89

Johann Otto Hoch 92

Anthony Kirkland 95

Adam Leroy Lane 98

James Marlow & Cynthia Coffman 101

Lee Roy Martin 105

David Mason 108

David Maust 111

Kenneth McDuff 114

David Meirhofer 118

Frederick Mors 121

Gerald Parker 124

Harry Powers 127

David Parker Ray 130

Efren Saldivar 133

Altemio Sanchez 136

Heriberto Seda 139

Anthony Allen Shore 142

Daniel Siebert 145

Jack Spillman III 148

James Swann 152

John Floyd Thomas, Jr. 155

Chester Turner 158

Faryion Wardrip..162
Karl Warner 165
John Francis Wille 168

50 American Serial Killers

In any field of human endeavor, there is a hierarchy, an unspoken ranking system where some individuals achieve greater renown than others. The field of serial murder is no different. Just about everyone has heard of the likes of Ted Bundy, John Wayne Gacy, and Jeffrey Dahmer. Their horrific crimes have bestowed upon them near legendary status. They are the vampires and werewolves of the age, flesh-and-blood monsters, all-American bogeymen.

Most serial killers, however, never achieve such lasting infamy. How many people, for example, have heard of Chester Turner, slayer and mutilator of at least 11 prostitutes and one of L.A.'s most prolific killers? How many have heard of Dana Sue Gray, a unique female serial killer who battered, stabbed and choked her elderly victims to death? Or Harry Powers, a depraved psychopath who got his jollies torturing lovelorn spinsters?

I would wager, not many.

And yet, the likes of Turner, Gray, and Powers are just as evil, their crimes every bit as depraved, vicious and repellent as those of their more celebrated brethren. And there are many more like them.

Howard Arthur Allen

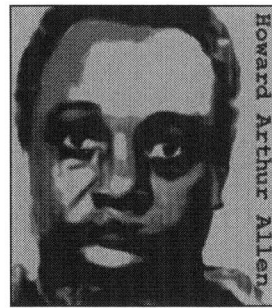

Serial killers, by their nature, prey on the weak and defenseless. Women and children are commonly targeted, but among the most heartless of killers are those who attack the frail and elderly. Howard Arthur Allen was one such creature, a heinous thug who savagely beat, stabbed and strangled at least three elderly victims to death.

Allen's first known murder was committed in August 1974, when he was 24 years old. On that occasion, he broke into the home of 85-year-old Opal Cooper, beating her to death in the course of a petty robbery. He was soon arrested for that murder, but the charge was reduced to manslaughter, and the sentence was a mere two to twenty-one years.

Allen would serve roughly half the maximum sentence before being paroled in January 1985. He returned to Indianapolis, where he found work at a car wash. For a while, he seemed to stay out of trouble. But the rage inside Howard Arthur Allen had not been extinguished. Before long, it flared up and he was hunting again.

On May 18, 1987, a 73-year-old Indianapolis woman narrowly escaped death after being choked and beaten by a prowler who broke into her home. Two days later another senior, 87-year-old Laverne Hale, was attacked, dying from her injuries on May 29.

On June 2, a burglar ransacked the home of an elderly man, just five blocks from the scene of the Hale murder. Fortunately for the tenant, he was not home. The killer vented his rage instead on the residence, setting it on fire.

Less than two weeks later, on July 14, 73-year-old Ernestine Griffin was murdered in her home near 57th and Keystone in Indianapolis. In the most brutal attack yet, the killer repeatedly plunged a ten-inch butcher knife into the frail woman, then caved in her skull with a toaster. His take from this carnage was a paltry fifteen dollars and a cheap camera belonging to the victim.

But Allen had made a crucial mistake. Days before the attack, he had called on Mrs. Griffin to enquire about a car her neighbor had for sale. Griffin had asked him to leave a number for her to pass on to the neighbor and Allen had done so. Now, as police processed the crime scene, they found that note, sitting on a kitchen counter.

Pulled in for questioning, Allen initially denied writing the note (a handwriting expert would later verify the handwriting as his) but after several hours of questioning, he finally admitted that he had been to Griffin's home. He even admitted punching her after (he said) she cussed him.

Finally, he all but admitted to the murder, saying, "I didn't stab the old lady, but if I did, I need help."

Then one of Allen's co-workers at the car wash came forward with a vital piece of evidence. He told investigators that on the day after the murder, Allen had given him a camera to stash in his locker. The camera was linked to Ernestine Griffin by its serial number and the film still in the camera belonged to Griffin.

Allen was indicted on charges of battery, burglary, and unlawful confinement. He was also charged with arson and burglary relating to the June 2 incident, as well as the murder of Ernestine Griffin.

A number of trials followed. In the spring of 1988, Allen was sentenced to 88 years for burglary and felony battery. In June of that year, he was sentenced to death for the murder of Ernestine Griffin.

Allen is currently incarcerated on death row in Indiana. He remains the prime suspect in eleven other murders of elderly victims, all of them attacked in their homes in and around Indianapolis.

Amy Archer-Gilligan

Widely considered America's most prolific female serial killer, Amy Archer-Gilligan was born in October 1868 in Litchfield, Connecticut, the eighth of ten children.

Very little is known of Archer-Gilligan's childhood. In 1897, she married James Archer and bore him a daughter, Mary, in December of that year. In 1901, the Archers were hired to care for an elderly man named John Seymour. When Seymour died in 1904, his relatives turned his Newington, Connecticut, home into a boarding house for the elderly. They kept James and Amy on as caretakers.

When Seymour's heirs decided to sell the house in 1907, the Archers moved to Windsor, Connecticut. There, they used their savings to buy a residential property, which they converted into a nursing home, the "Archer Home for the Elderly and Infirm."

Three years later, in 1910, James Archer died, apparently of Bright's disease. Amy had taken out a life insurance policy on James just a few weeks prior to his death. The payout enabled her to keep running the nursing home.

In 1913, Amy married Michael W. Gilligan, a wealthy widower with four adult sons. The marriage was short-lived. Michael died on February 20, 1914, leaving his entire estate to Amy. The official cause of death was "acute bilious attack."

Now financially secure, Archer-Gilligan was free to run her nursing home, which she did, despite growing unease at the high number of deaths among her residents. Granted, they were elderly, and the 12 deaths recorded between 1907 and 1910, seemed reasonable. However, between 1911 and 1916, 48 people died in Archer-Gilligan's care. Unsurprisingly, suspicious relatives began asking questions.

Matters eventually came to a head on May 29, 1914, with the death of Franklin R. Andrews. On the day he died, Andrews had appeared in good health and had spent the morning working in the garden. However, during the afternoon his health rapidly deteriorated and by evening he was dead. The official cause of death was a gastric ulcer.

Franklin Andrews' personal papers passed to his sister Nellie Pierce, who noticed that Archer-Gilligan had been pressing Andrews for money and that Andrews had recently signed over a substantial sum to her. In fact, Mrs. Pierce discovered on further investigation that a number of Archer-Gilligan's residents died not long after bequeathing large sums to their caregiver.

Pierce took her suspicions to the district attorney. When he ignored her, she took her story to the local newspaper, The Hartford Courant. On May 9, 1916, the Courant published the first of several articles on Archer-Gilligan's "Murder Factory." The articles caused such a public outcry that the police were forced to act.

Yet even now, they kept their inquiries low-key. A year passed before the bodies of Michael Gilligan, Franklin Andrews, and three other boarders were exhumed. All showed signs of either arsenic or strychnine poisoning. As police inquiries continued, they learned that Archer-Gilligan had been buying large quantities of arsenic, ostensibly to kill rats. They also discovered that Michael Gilligan's will was a forgery, drafted in Amy's handwriting.

Archer-Gilligan was arrested and tried for murder. On June 18, 1917, she was found guilty on a single charge, for the murder of Franklin Andrews. She was sentenced to death but was subsequently given a new trial in 1919. On this occasion, she entered an insanity plea, citing her addiction to morphine. She was nonetheless found guilty of second-degree murder and sentenced to life in prison.

In 1924, Archer-Gilligan was declared insane and transferred to the Connecticut Hospital for the Insane in Middletown. She remained there until her death on April 23, 1962.

Benjamin Atkins

Like many serial killers, Benjamin Atkins did not have the best start in life. The child of an absent father and a crack-addicted prostitute mother, Atkins grew up mainly in boys' homes and institutions. During the brief periods that he was in his mother's care, she would take him out on the streets with her and make him sit in the backseat of cars while she engaged in sex in the front. As a 10-year-old, Atkins was raped by one of his mother's clients, so it is unsurprising that he grew up with an abiding hatred of prostitutes and prostitution.

Eventually, that hatred exploded in a nine-month killing spree during which he claimed 11 victims. According to the FBI, no other American serial killer has claimed as many victims in such a short time span.

All of the victims were killed in Detroit, Michigan (primarily in the Highland Park area) between December 1991 and August 1992. All were raped and strangled, their bodies dumped in vacant buildings. Most were working prostitutes. Many were drug addicts.

As the body count mounted, Detroit PD, the Michigan State Police, and the FBI pulled together to form a task force. But, as so often happens in cases of serial murder, it was the victim that got away that led to Atkins downfall.

Darlene Saunders, 35, was attacked and raped in October 1991, in Highland Park. Atkins left her for dead, but she survived and was able to identify her attacker as a man she knew only as "Tony."

Atkins was arrested while walking along Woodward Avenue, in an area where many of the bodies had been dumped. Brought in for questioning, he initially denied the charges, claiming he was homosexual and had no interest in women. However, Detroit homicide detective, Sgt. Ronald Sanders, managed to win his confidence and eventually Atkins confessed to the murders, including one victim whose body had not yet been found. Asked why he had done it, Atkins told investigators: "I killed all 11 of them so I didn't have to worry about them pressing charges."

About the murder of one of his victims, 23-year-old Juanita Harvey, he added: "After raping her, having sex, and hating her for being a woman, I had the desire to kill her. I just wanted to hate her and cause her harm."

Atkins went on trial in October 1993. There was never any real doubt as to his guilt, but public defender, Jeffrey Edison, fought hard to convince jurors to show compassion, citing Atkins' harsh upbringing and his drug dependency. It was to no avail. Atkins was found guilty and sentenced to 11 life terms.

He would serve only four years of his sentence. Atkins died at the Duane Waters Hospital in Jackson, Michigan, on September 17, 1997. Cause of death was listed as "complications arising from HIV infection." He was 29 years old.

Speaking after his death, trial prosecutor, Michael Reynolds said: "While no one takes joy in another's death, even one who has committed such hideous crimes, at least those who lost loved ones at Mr. Atkins' hands can take comfort in knowing he will never be released back into society."

Jake Bird

Jake Bird had a stock answer for anyone who asked where he was from. "Somewhere out in Louisiana where they ain't got no post office," he'd say. Wherever that town was, Jake remained there until he was 19-years-old. Then he hit the road and would remain a transient for the rest of his life.

Work was plentiful in those days for anyone with the strength and stamina to wield a pick, a sledgehammer or a shovel. Jake found employment as a manual laborer on road crews and on the railroads. It was tough, backbreaking work, but it built up his strength and allowed him to travel the country in search of recreation.

And recreation to Jake Bird meant rape and murder. By the time of his capture in 1947, he'd racked up 44 victims, one for each year of his life.

The double homicide that would eventually end Jake Bird's murderous career occurred on October 30, 1947. On that day, Bird was scouting a neighborhood in Tacoma, Washington, when he spotted 52-year-old Bertha Kludt and decided to attack her.

Finding an ax in the woodshed, Bird stripped off his clothes and entered the home where he raped Mrs. Kludt before hacking her and her 17-year-old daughter, Beverley, to death.

Unfortunately for Bird, the victims' dying screams were heard by a neighbor, who called the police. Officers Andrew P. Sabutis and Evan "Skip" Davies were dispatched to the scene and immediately encountered a barefoot man running from the house. The two patrolmen gave chase, eventually trapping Bird in an alley. Seeing that he was cornered Bird pull a knife and attacked the officers, cutting Davies' hand and stabbing Sabutis in the shoulder. Sabutis, though, was a former prizefighter, and a left hook to the jaw soon put Bird's lights out. The officers then returned to the house where they found the two women, brutally slain.

Bird's trial was set for Monday, November 24, 1947. As was customary in those days, he was charged with only one murder, that of Bertha Kludt. The logic was that, should he somehow be found not guilty, he could then be tried for the other murder.

Of course, there was never any prospect that Bird, a black man who'd murdered two white women, would be found not guilty. After a trial lasting just one-and-a-half days, he was convicted and sentenced to hang.

Unlike the modern era, where condemned prisoners can sit for years or even decades on death row, justice moved swiftly in those days. It was rare for an execution to be delayed by more than a couple of months. But Bird and his lawyer played the system well. Through a series of stays and reprieves, they managed to delay the inevitable for nearly two years.

Many of those stays were achieved by offering to clear up unsolved homicides. During that time, Bird confessed to 44 murders and was visited by law enforcement officers from all over the country. At least 11 murders were definitely attributed to him, occurring in locations as far flung as Evanston, Illinois; Louisville, Kentucky; Omaha, Nebraska; Kansas City, Kansas; Sioux Falls, South Dakota; Cleveland, Ohio; Orlando, Florida; and Portage, Wisconsin.

In addition, police in Houston suspected Bird in the murder of a Mrs. Richardson, and Chicago authorities believed him responsible for a weighted body retrieved from Lake Michigan, near Kenosha. Los Angeles detectives wanted to question Bird about the murder of a black youth and a Jewish grocer, while in New York City, he was linked to the robbery and murder of a delicatessen owner.

Bird's favored targets, though, were women, specifically white women. A psychiatrist who examined him in prison said that Bird derived sexual satisfaction from the sight of women cowering from him in terror.

Time eventually ran out for Jake Bird in July 1949. On Thursday, July 14, he ate his final meal and spoke with his attorney for two hours. Later that night, he was moved to a holding cell, where he shaved and dressed in a new suit.

Just after midnight, he was marched ten feet from the death cell to the gallows. Prison chaplain, Reverend Arvid Ohrnell, started to read a note from Bird, saying he bore no malice toward anyone and sought forgiveness. Before he had finished, the trapdoor was sprung, and Jake Bird plunged to his death.

Dallen Bounds

On Saturday, June 26, 1999, officers from the Greenville Police Department in South Carolina were called to the scene of a brutal murder at the local Radio Shack outlet. Employee Jonathan Lemuel Lara had been found dead in a storeroom, his hands tied with flex, a screwdriver protruding from a fatal neck wound. The killer had left through a back door after locking the store, turning off the lights and hanging a closed sign in the window. There was no sign of a struggle.

Nearly six months later, a deliveryman arrived at a small flower shop in Greenville to check on the clerk, Karen Moore Hayden, who was not answering the phone. He found the store in darkness, a closed sign in the window. This was odd, so the man phoned the police. They found the 30-year-old clerk in a back storage room, lying face down in a pool of her own blood. Her throat had been slashed.

The crime bore startling similarities to the Radio Shack murder. As in that case, the victim was left in a storeroom and the killer had turned out the lights and locked up. The store appeared undisturbed, with no signs of a struggle.

Early the next morning, Pickens County Sheriff's deputies responded to a 911 call from a residence on Antioch Road. There they found Sandra Ott, lying on the kitchen floor with a gunshot wound to her head. Ott's ex-husband, Timothy, had apparently fled to a neighbor's house to call the police, but the killer had followed him there and shot him in the head after breaking in through the living room window. The neighbor was found cowering in a closet. The Ott's 5-year-old son was found fast asleep in his bed.

The police, at least, had an I.D. on the shooter. He was 28-year-old Dallen Forrest Bounds, Sandra Ott's current boyfriend. Within the next 12 hours, Sheriff's deputies tracked him to a house on South Third Street in Easley where he had taken two women hostage. A tense standoff ensued, ending when Bounds put a pistol to his head and blew his brains out.

The day after the double homicide, Greenville police received an anonymous tip-off linking Bounds to the murders of Jonathan Lara and Karen Hayden. Subsequent forensic evidence proved this to be the case.

Bounds is also a suspect in three unsolved murders in the state of Washington.

Judy Buenoano

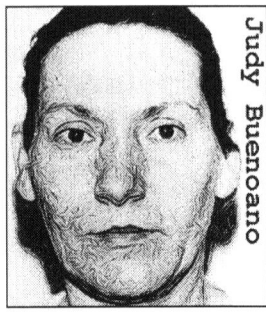

Judy Buenoano was born Judias Welty, in Quanah, Texas, on April 4, 1943. Her father was an itinerant farm worker, her mother a full-blooded Apache, who died of tuberculosis when Judy was just two years old.

After her mother's death, Judy lived for a time with her grandparents before being reunited with her father in Roswell, New Mexico. Judy and her brother, Robert, suffered years of physical abuse at their father's hands until eventually, at 14, Judy snapped and struck back. That earned her 60 days jail time and a posting to a reform school in Albuquerque, New Mexico.

Graduating in 1959, she returned to Roswell and found work as a nurse's aide. On March 30, 1961, she gave birth to an illegitimate son who she named Michael. Less than a year later, in January

1962, she married air force officer, James Goodyear. She bore him two children, James Jr. and Kimberly, while James Goodyear adopted Judy's son, Michael.

By 1967, Judy was living in Orlando, Florida, while her husband was serving in Vietnam. He completed his final tour of duty in 1971 but was back just three months when he was admitted to hospital suffering from vomiting and dizzy spells. He died on September 15, 1971, leaving Judy to collect the proceeds of three life insurance policies. Another insurance payout followed before year's end, after Judy's Orlando house burned down. Her take this time was $90,000.

In 1972, Judy moved her family to Pensacola, Florida, where she shacked up with a new lover, Bobby Joe Morris. When Morris moved to Trinidad, Colorado, in 1977, Judy went with him. But not before collecting insurance on another house fire.

They'd been in Colorado less than a year when Bobby Joe was admitted to San Rafael Hospital. Doctors could find no cause for his sudden illness, but he died on January 28, his death put down to a heart attack. In early February, Judy cashed three insurance policies on his life.

On May 3, 1978, Judy legally changed her last name to Buenoano (the Spanish equivalent of Goodyear) in an apparent tribute to her late husband. A month later, she moved her family back to Pensacola.

In 1979, Michael dropped out of school and joined the army. After completing basic training he was posted to Fort Benning, Georgia, but before taking up that post, he stopped off to visit his mother in Florida. By the time he reported at Fort Benning on November 6, 1979, he was already grievously ill and army doctors found seven times the normal level of arsenic in his body. Despite six weeks of intensive care, the muscles of his arms and lower legs had atrophied to the point where Michael could neither walk nor use his hands. There was little doctors could do to reverse the damage. He received a medical discharge and left the hospital wearing braces and a prosthetic device on his arm.

On May 13, 1980, Michael, his mother and younger brother were canoeing on the East River, near Milton, Florida, when their boat overturned. James and Judy made it safely to shore, but Michael drowned. Judy received a $20,000 payout from the army as well as the proceeds of two policies on Michael's life.

She used her latest windfall to open a beauty parlor and began dating Pensacola businessman, John Gentry II. In October 1982, the couple took out life insurance policies on one another. Unbeknownst to Gentry, Judy later upped his coverage from $50,000 to $500,000, paying the premiums herself.

On December 16, Gentry was hospitalized after suffering dizzy spells and chronic vomiting. He was released 12 days later and the symptoms disappeared once he stopped taking the vitamin pills Judy had been feeding him.

On June 25, 1983, Gentry left a dinner party early to pick up some champagne. As he turned the ignition of his car, it exploded leaving him with severe injuries, his life barely saved by trauma surgeons. Detectives investigating the incident soon learned of the insurance policy on his life and also found out about Gentry's mysterious illness the previous year. An analysis of the pills he'd taken revealed that they contained the poison paraformaldehyde.

On July 27, federal agents searched Judy's home and found wire and tape that matched the Gentry car bomb. They were also able to trace the dynamite used in the bomb and in mid-August Judy was charged with attempted murder.

Murder charges followed in the deaths of Michael Buenoano, Bobby Joe Morris and James Goodyear, for which she was eventually sentenced to death. She was also suspected in the murder of another lover, Gerald Dossett.

Judy Buenoano was put to death in Florida's electric chair on March 30, 1998.

Dean Philip Carter

By some definitions, Dean Carter would be considered a spree killer, rather than a serial killer, such was the murderous explosion of violence that he unleashed. Born in Nome, Alaska, on August 30, 1955, Carter was the illegitimate son of a half-Eskimo woman. He was put up for adoption at birth, and taken in by the former police chief of Nome.

However, the law-enforcement background of young Dean's adoptive father did nothing to curb the boy's youthful excesses. By the age of 12, he'd been declared a juvenile delinquent and committed to a camp for youthful offenders, an institution he escaped from three times. He would later be placed in a foster home, but continued to commit crimes. By 15, he was an experienced burglar and as a young adult he did time in Oregon for auto theft and in Alaska for burglary.

On his release from this latest prison term, Carter seemed determined to get his life together. He studied to be a cameraman and found work with KTUU-TV in Anchorage, Alaska. In the early eighties, he moved to Seattle, Washington, where he continued as a freelancer in his chosen profession.

In the spring of 1984, Carter decided to move to California. But his quest for new beginnings would bring a nightmare end to at least five women as he suddenly ran amok in a six-week orgy of rape and murder.

As Carter continues to profess his innocence of the crimes, no one knows what triggered his killing spree. What is known, is that on March 25, 1984, Carter attacked and raped a San Diego woman. That victim survived, but roommates Jillette Mills, 35, and Susan Knoll, 33, were not so lucky. They were murdered on April 10, their bodies stuffed into a closet at their Culver City apartment.

The following day, in Los Angeles, Carter strangled 24-year-old Bonnie Guthrie, a friend of Susan Knoll's. Then, on April 13, he raped and killed 37-year-old Tok Chum Kim in her Oakland apartment. A day later, he was in San Diego, where he strangled 25-year-old Janette Cullins to death at her home.

Given the rate at which these rape / murders were committed it is frightening to think how many victims Dean Carter might have taken. Fortunately, he was arrested on May 15, in Ventura County, and despite his protestations of innocence, was held in lieu of a $1 million bond while detectives built their case.

There was plenty of physical evidence linking him to the crimes. His semen was found inside the bodies of three of the murder victims; his bloody palm print was found in one of the victims' homes; and there was an ATM video showing him drawing money from another victim's bank account. In addition, a car that he stole from his first murder victim was found a block from another victim's home. And if that were not enough, he was found in possession of personal effects taken from the homes of each of the victims.

Carter was tried and convicted of the murders as well as two rapes in which the victims survived. He was sentenced to death and currently awaits execution on California's death row at San Quentin.

Joseph Christopher

Joseph Christopher was a racially motivated serial killer who launched a private, one-man war against African Americans and Hispanics in September 1980, a killing spree that left 14 victims dead, countless others injured.

Christopher's war began on September 22, when he shot 14-year-old Glenn Dunn, as he sat in a stolen car outside a Buffalo supermarket. Eyewitnesses described the assailant as a "white youth." The following day, 32-year-old Harold Green was shot at a fast-food restaurant in Cheektowaga. That night, Emmanuel Thomas, 30, was shot and killed near his home by an unidentified sniper. A fourth victim, Joseph McCoy, was shot and killed on September 24, in the nearby town of Niagara Falls.

Investigators were by now aware that they were hunting a serial killer, as all four victims were killed with the same .22-caliber weapon. In short order, the press had dubbed HIM the ".22-Caliber Killer."

As word spread of a white killer targeting blacks, sporadic violence flared up with incidents of blacks pelting white motorists with rocks. Rumors that a racist paramilitary group was behind the killings did nothing to calm the situation.

And still, the murders continued. On October 8, 71-year-old taxi-driver, Parler Edwards, was found in the trunk of his car, his heart crudely hacked from his chest. The following day, another black cab driver, 40-year-old Ernest Jones, was found beside the Niagara River with his heart ripped out.

The killer next struck at a Buffalo hospital on October 10. 37-year-old Collin Cole was attacked in his bed by a white assailant, who told him: "I hate niggers," before attempting to strangle him. Fortunately, the arrival of a nurse saved Cole's life. Her description of the attacker matched eyewitness reports of the .22-Caliber Killer.

There were no further attacks during the next six weeks, but on December 22, an unknown assailant unleashed a 13-hour killing spree in Manhattan, New York City, claiming four victims - three African American and one Hispanic.

Luis Rodriguez, a 19-year-old courier, was stabbed to death at around 3:30 p.m. in what was at first believed to be a holdup. 30-year-old Antone Davis was knifed to death at around 6:50 p.m. Richard Renner, 20, died less than four hours later. The final

Manhattan victim was an unidentified black man, stabbed to death on a street near Madison Square Garden.

On December 29, 1980, the man dubbed the "Midtown Slasher" by the NYPD, was back in Buffalo, where he stabbed 31-year-old Roger Adams to death.

And he wasn't done yet. Wendell Barnes, 26, was killed in Rochester on December 30, while Albert Menefee was lucky to survive a wound that narrowly missed his heart.

On January 1, Larry Little and Calvin Crippen survived separate attacks, while on January 6, police announced that the stabbings were probably linked to the .22-caliber shootings.

Twelve days later, at Fort Benning Georgia, military police arrested a private named Joseph Christopher for a knife attack on a black soldier. A search of Christopher's residence turned up a gun barrel, two rifle stocks and a quantity of .22-caliber ammunition. Investigators also learned that Christopher had arrived at Fort Benning from upstate New York shortly after the .22-caliber attacks ended there and that he'd been AWOL in New York City at the time of the Manhattan attacks.

In May 1981, Christopher was charged with four fatal shootings in Buffalo. Indictments soon followed for the New York City murders. In October 1981, Christopher waived his right to a jury trial in Buffalo. Two months later, he was found mentally incompetent for trial, although that ruling was later overturned and he was convicted on three counts of first-degree murder and sentenced to a prison term of 60 years to life.

In July 1985, Christopher's Buffalo conviction was overturned on grounds that the judge had improperly barred testimony indicating mental incompetence. Three months later, a Manhattan jury rejected his insanity plea and convicted him of the murder of Luis Rodriguez. He was sentenced to life imprisonment.

Juan Covington

Most serial killers are psychopaths, lethal predators who derive pleasure from their deadly acts. Juan Covington, by comparison, was diagnosed a schizopath, a rare breed of killer who targets people who he believes mean to do him harm.

Covington grew up in a working-class neighborhood of Logan, Pennsylvania. He attended a Roman Catholic school and enjoyed basketball and hanging out with his older brother, James, who he idolized. After graduating high school, he tried college but soon dropped out. In May 1983, he was hired as a bus driver by SEPTA, a job he'd hold until 2001.

In 1985, Covington began dating a Temple University student. The woman eventually moved in with Covington and bore him a son, Joe, in 1986, although the couple never married.

In the late 80s, Covington sought mental health treatment at a local hospital. Then, after the death of his father in 1989, he went into deep depression and started displaying worryingly erratic behavior.

Covington's family urged him to see a psychiatrist in the early 90s and although he complied, he became withdrawn, refusing to care for his mother while she was suffering from advanced diabetes. In 1993, Covington suddenly announced to his family that he was cured and was stopping his medication. Privately, he told his brother that the medicines were "turning him into the devil."

As his paranoid symptoms intensified, his son's mother ended their relationship and moved out, taking the boy with her. Covington moved in briefly with another woman, but by 1997 he was back at his parents' home. His mother had since died and Covington found himself alone in the house, which he soon emptied of furniture, giving it all to a neighbor, Harold Belcher.

At around this time, Covington became obsessed with a fellow bus driver, Brenwanda Smith. He asked her for a date, but she turned him down. Soon after she disappeared. Although there is no proof that Covington was involved in her disappearance, he remains the prime suspect.

There is little doubt, though, regarding his next victim. The Rev. Thomas Lee Devlin (Covington's cousin) was gunned down in the basement of a Logan home in August 1998. When Covington eventually confessed to the murder, he said he'd killed Devlin because "he had the power to wipe me off the face of the earth." He also claimed Devlin had used witchcraft to swell his gums and cause pus to pour out of his forehead.

By September 2001, Covington's life was spiraling out of control. Fired from his job at SEPTA because of constant altercations with co-workers, he found work at a Home Depot store. That didn't last long. After punching a customer in the face, his employment was terminated.

In May 2003, David Stewart, a friend of Covington's neighbor Harold Belcher, was shot eight times as he walked to work. Covington later confessed to the shooting, saying that he woke up that morning and decided, "I'm gonna kill someone today." He then walked outside and shot the first person he saw.

Early in 2004, Covington shot and gravely wounded another man, William Bryant. Then, in May 2005, he shot and killed Odies Bosket. Bosket was shot three times near the entrance to the Logan subway station as he rushed to pick up his daughter from day-care. Although he lived just blocks away from Covington, the two men did not know each other.

After Covington was fired from Home Depot, he found work at Stericycle, a company that handles the removal of hospital waste. It was in this capacity that he met his next victim, Trish McDermott, an X-ray technician at Pennsylvania Hospital.

In the early hours of May 17, 2005, Covington followed McDermott as she was on her way to work. After stalking her from a bus stop, he walked up behind her and shot her in the back of the head. He'd later insist that McDermott had been trying to kill him with a CAT-scan machine. The machine in question turned out to be an office photocopier.

Unfortunately for Covington, the murder of Trish McDermott was captured by a hospital surveillance camera. He was arrested at his home on July 12, 2005, and later sentenced to three life terms, one for each murder.

Andre Crawford

The police knew they were looking for a serial killer, an unnamed slayer who had been genetically linked to the murders of seven prostitutes in the Englewood and New City areas of Chicago. But their quarry remained elusive, had escaped their grasp for six, long years. Then, in January 2000, several tips caused investigators to hone in on 37-year-old Andre Crawford, an unemployed man who did odd jobs around the neighborhood.

Crawford was brought in for questioning and quickly confessed to the seven murders of which he was suspected. He then shocked investigators by admitting to three more killings that had not previously been connected to him. Another prostitute murder would later be added to the charge sheet, bringing his final tally to 11.

The killer's modus operandi was simple. He lured the women from the streets to abandoned buildings with the promise of drugs in exchange for sexual favors. If the woman agreed to have sex before receiving her payoff, he'd simply cheat her by refusing to hand over the drugs once the deed was done. If, however, she insisted on payment up front or if she resisted him, he'd choke her into unconsciousness, then rape her before strangling her to death. On one occasion, Crawford confessed, he had sex with a victim after she was dead. He enjoyed the act of necrophilia so much that he hid the body so that he could return to it later.

Crawford was well known in New City and Englewood. He grew up in the neighborhood and had at various times lived in abandoned buildings in the area. Unsurprisingly, these sites are where several of the bodies were discovered. Crawford also knew a number of his victims.

Katrina Martin, a former prostitute and recovering drug addict was one of three people who passed Crawford's name on to the police. She had known Crawford since 1992, when she lived with a man who allowed crack addicts to get high in his apartment. Crawford was a regular there, as were Patricia Dunns, Tommie Dennis, Sonja Brandon, Constance Bailey, Sheryl Johnson and Shaquanta Langley – 6 of his 11 victims.

Yet even as Crawford fraternized with prostitutes, he was scathing in his criticism of them, telling anyone who would listen that they, "shouldn't be out there, they should get a job and do something better with their lives." On another occasion, he told Katrina Martin that prostitutes deserved to die. "They need to be strangled and have their heads beaten in," she remembers him saying. It was then that she decided to pass his name on to the police.

Crawford was arrested on January 28, 2000. He expressed his relief at being captured, stating that: "I was glad I was caught because I was like a shark in a pool." Nonetheless, he entered not guilty pleas at his trial in December 2009.

Crawford's protestations of innocence were to no avail. DNA evidence linked him to all of the victims. He was spared the death penalty only because the jury could not reach a unanimous decision, with one juror voting against.

Andre Crawford is currently serving life in prison without the possibility of parole.

Brian Dugan

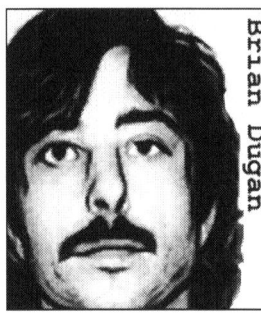

Brian Dugan was born in Nashua, New Hampshire on September 23, 1956, the second child of alcoholic parents. As a child he was a chronic bed wetter, a fire starter and a torturer of animals, thus displaying all three of the triad of behaviors commonly associated with fledgling serial killers.

In 1972, with the family now living in Lisle, Illinois, Brian ran away to Iowa where he was arrested on a burglary charge. Other arrests soon followed, for arson, battery, and various robberies. In 1974, he attempted to abduct a 10-year-old girl from a train station in Lisle. Charges were eventually dropped although Dugan continued to offend, resulting in his eventual incarceration at the Menard Correctional Center from 1979 to 1982.

Within a year of his release, Duggan had committed his first murder. On February 25, 1983, 10-year-old Jeanine Nicarico was abducted from her home in Naperville, Illinois. Her battered body was found two days later, six miles away. She had been raped and beaten to death.

The police soon made an arrest, taking into custody Rolando Cruz, Alejandro Hernandez and Stephen Buckley, three gang members from Aurora, Illinois. Cruz and Hernandez were eventually convicted and sentenced to death, but unfortunately, the real killer was still out there. On July 15, 1984, he struck again.

Dugan was driving in his car when he stopped alongside Donna Schnorr, a pretty 27-year-old nurse from Geneva, Illinois. He followed Schnorr until they reached a deserted stretch of highway, then forced her off the road with his car. He then pulled the terrified woman from her vehicle, beat and raped her and then drowned her in a quarry.

Dugan had now gotten away with two murders and like most serial killers he was probably becoming cocky in his ability to evade capture. It drove him on to greater depravity, culminating in a deadly crime spree in mid-1985. On May 6, 1985, Dugan raped a 21-year-old woman, who was fortunate to escape with her life. On May 28, he failed in an attempt to snatch a 19-year-old from the street, but a day later he abducted and brutally raped a 16-year-old girl.

On June 2, 1985, Dugan encountered 7-year-old Melissa Ackerman and 8-year-old Opal Horton, riding their bikes in Somonauk, Illinois. He grabbed Opal first and forced her into his car. Then he went after Melissa, during which time Opal managed to escape.

Melissa was not so lucky. Her body was found several weeks later. She'd been raped and then drowned in a creek.

On the day of the Ackerman murder, Dugan had been pulled over by a police officer in Somonauk, who had noticed his out-of-date license sticker. Then, after Opal Horton gave a description of both Dugan and his vehicle, police officers put the strands together and Dugan was soon under arrest. With strong physical evidence linking him to Melissa Ackerman's murder, Dugan took the deal on offer, pleading guilty to the Ackerman and Schnorr murders in order to avoid the death penalty. He offered no explanation for the crimes, saying only: "It might have been for the sex, but I don't understand why. I wish I knew why I did a lot of things, but I don't."

Dugan may have escaped death by lethal injection but he was still afraid that he might be linked to Jeanine Nicarico's murder. He therefore approached prosecutors offering a confession in exchange for life in prison. The move backfired when prosecutors refused the deal, but re-opened the case anyway.

Rolando Cruz and Alejandro Hernandez were eventually exonerated of the murder after DNA evidence linked Dugan to the crime. He was indicted in 2005 and, in 2009, sentenced to death.

It was a sentence that would never be carried out. In 2011, Illinois governor Patrick Quinn abolished capital punishment and Dugan's sentence was commuted to life in prison without the possibility of parole.

Edward Wayne Edwards

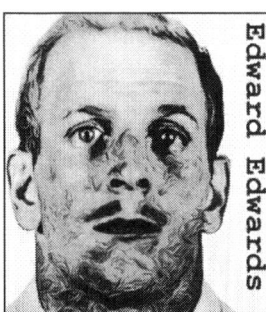

When he was still a child, Edward Edwards told a nun that he wanted to be a criminal; as an older man, he described himself as a cross between Don Juan and John Dillinger. Desperate to be famous, Edwards once committed a string of armed robberies without wearing a mask. His greatest achievement, he said, was making it onto the FBI's Ten Most Wanted list.

Edwards did not have the best start in life. He was just two years old when his mother committed suicide and he was sent to an orphanage in Parma, Ohio. That was in 1940. By 1948 he'd been committed to reform school in Pennsylvania. Returning to Akron, Ohio, in 1950, he quickly fell into the criminal lifestyle, committing a string of burglaries.

In late 1950, he enlisted in the Marines, but his military career would be a short and undistinguished one. After going AWOL from

Camp Lejeune, North Carolina, he was arrested in Jacksonville, Florida and dishonorably discharged. Over the next decade, Edwards was in and out of prison on a catalog of charges, ranging from federal interstate transportation violations to burglary and armed robbery. He also proved to be an accomplished escape artist, breaking out of penitentiaries in Akron and in Portland, Oregon.

In 1960, he was questioned in connection with the double homicide of a young couple. Soon after, he went on the run after fraudulently cashing some checks. While on the lam, Edwards committed a number of daring armed robberies, which saw him elevated to the FBI's 10 Most Wanted fugitives list in November 1961. On January 20, 1962, he was captured in Atlanta, Georgia, and in May of that year, he drew a 16-year term at the Federal Penitentiary in Leavenworth.

Edwards was paroled in 1967, and appeared a changed man, touring as a motivational speaker and, in 1971, publishing a book on his rehabilitation.

In 1977, while Edwards was living in Doylestown, Ohio, Billy Lavaco, 21, and Judy Straub, 18, were gunned down with a shotgun, their bodies found in Silver Creek Park in nearby Norton. Edwards was not suspected of the murders.

In 1980, another double homicide occurred, this time in Wisconsin. Tim Hack and Kelly Drew, both 19, went missing after they attended a wedding reception at a hall where Edwards worked as a handyman. Their bodies were found a short while later. Drew had been raped and strangled while Hack had been stabbed to death. Edwards was questioned in connection with the murders but denied any involvement. A short while later he left the state and moved to Pennsylvania.

In December 1982, Edwards burned down a house he was renting and was convicted of arson. He drew a four-year prison term and was released in July 1986.

Edwards committed his last known murder in May 1996, when he shot his 25-year-old foster son, Dannie Boy Edwards, in order to collect on a life insurance policy. Dannie's skeletal remains were found by a hunter, buried in a shallow grave near Troy Cemetery, less than a mile from Edwards' home. Edwards was questioned about the murder but denied complicity.

And he might well have gotten away with the murders had it not been for the advent of DNA technology. In 2007, Wisconsin investigators submitted a semen sample taken from Kelly Drew for analysis. They matched that sample to Edward Edwards in June 2009.

On July 30, 2009, Edwards was arrested at his home in Louisville, Kentucky, and charged with the murders of Timothy Hack and Kelly Drew. He quickly confessed, admitting also to the double homicide of Billy Lavaco and Judy Straub, and to the murder of his foster son.

Edwards was sentenced to death in May 2011, for the murder of Dannie Boy Edwards. He died in prison of natural causes before the sentence could be carried out.

Donald Leroy Evans

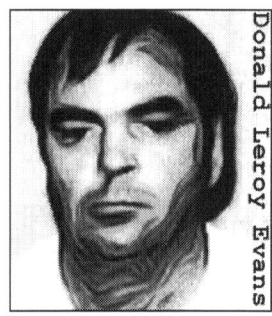

In August 1991, while the world's media was fixated on the heinous crimes committed by the "Milwaukee Cannibal," Jeffrey Dahmer, another serial killer was quietly taken into custody. The capture of a drifter named Donald Leroy Evans hardly merited a mention alongside the lurid Dahmer headlines. Yet if Evans' claim to 60 murders is true, he ranks among America's most prolific serial killers.

The case first came to light on August 12, 1991, when Evans was arrested by Louisiana police and immediately confessed to raping and strangling Beatrice Routh, a 10-year-old homeless girl who he'd abducted from a park in Gulfport, Mississippi, on August 1. Investigators were skeptical at first, until Evans led them to the body, left in a field beside a rural Mississippi highway. Evans was charged with the murder and then dropped another bombshell. He admitted to at least 60 murders, spanning two decades and 10 different states.

According to Evans, he started killing soon after being discharged from the Marines in 1970. Starting off in his hometown of Galveston, Texas, he began drifting from town to town, "killing folk" in every place he visited. What is more, he claimed that he could lead investigators to every single murder site.

The authorities were obviously interested in a confession that could potentially close many unsolved homicides. Yet they treated Evans' confessions with caution. The Henry Lee Lucas fiasco was still fresh in many people's minds. In that case, investigators had swallowed everything Lucas had to say, and been left embarrassed when many of those claims turned out to be false.

Yet, while Evans' confessions were almost certainly exaggerated, they seemed to carry a lot more credibility than those of Lucas. Certainly, Evans had not been fed information by overzealous cops, as Lucas had been. And in at least two murders, those of two Florida prostitutes, Evans was able to provide details that had not been reported in the media. In another Florida homicide, the strangulation death of Ira Jean Smith, he would later be tried and convicted in 1995.

First, though, he had to stand trial in Mississippi, for the murder of Beatrice Routh. During that trial, in June 1993, Evans escaped from the Harrison County jail. He was recaptured soon after, having covered less than a mile from the prison.

Evans had asked for the death penalty, and after the jury heard how he'd lured young Beatrice away from her mother with the promise of buying them food, they were happy to oblige.

Condemned to die, Evans was sent to the Mississippi State Penitentiary to await execution. There he shaved his head, declared himself a white supremacist and insisted on being called "Hi Hitler." He also recanted all of his earlier confessions.

On 5 January 1999, Evans was fatally stabbed by a fellow death row inmate, Jimmie Mack. He was 41 at the time of his death. He remains a strong suspect in 12 of the cases to which he confessed. However, the bulk of his claims have not been proven, and the cases remain unsolved.

Joseph Paul Franklin

Joseph Paul Franklin was born James Clayton Vaughn, Jr., in Mobile, Alabama. His father was an alcoholic drifter, who abandoned his family for long stretches at a time, his sporadic homecomings marked by physical and psychological abuse of his children.

When Franklin was in high school, he was involved in an accident that left him with severely impaired eyesight and meant that he escaped the draft and was not required to serve in Vietnam. He married in 1968, whereupon he appeared to undergo a personality change. He began beating his wife within weeks of the wedding and would regularly abuse her throughout their marriage. Around this time Franklin's previously all-white neighborhood was beginning to become racially integrated, and he began to adopt more extreme views, veering towards far-right ideologies.

In 1972, following his mother's death, he moved to Atlanta, where he joined the neo-fascist National States Rights Party, as well as the local Ku Klux Klan. Franklin was particularly antagonistic towards interracial couples. In one incident, on Labor Day 1976, he followed a couple and sprayed them with Mace.

Franklin legally changed his name in 1976, and soon after took to the road. He spent the years 1977 to 1980, roaming the South and Midwest on a killing spree that would claim at least 13 lives.

His deadly campaign began on July 29, 1977, when he bombed a synagogue in Chattanooga, Tennessee. Nine days later, he appeared in Madison, Wisconsin, where he shot and killed an interracial couple, Alphonse Manning and Toni Schwenn. On October 8, he launched a sniper attack on worshippers exiting a synagogue in St. Louis, Missouri, injuring two and killing Gerald Gordon.

Harold McIver was killed while working the night shift at a Doraville, Georgia, fast food restaurant on July 22, 1979. Three months later, in Oklahoma City, another interracial couple, Jesse Taylor and Marian Bresette, were shot to death.

Franklin launched two separate attacks in Indianapolis during January 1980, killing two black men. On May 3, he killed a young white woman, Rebecca Bergstrom, dumping her body near Tomah, Wisconsin. On June 8, he was in Cincinnati, where cousins Darrell Lane and Dante Brown were killed by sniper fire from a nearby railway bridge. A week later, Franklin gunned down a black couple in Johnstown, Pennsylvania, and on August 20, he shot joggers Ted Fields and David Martin in Salt Lake City, Utah.

Franklin was arrested in Kentucky on September 25, 1980. He escaped from custody, only to be recaptured a month later in Florida. Now state and federal officials were faced with the mammoth task of unraveling his deadly campaign and bringing him to justice.

In 1982, Franklin was acquitted of the May 1980 shooting of civil rights leader Vernon Jordan in Fort Wayne, Indiana. The reprieve was short-lived. He was found guilty of murder in Utah and sentenced to life imprisonment. While serving that term, Franklin confessed to the 1978 shooting that left Larry Flint, publisher of Hustler magazine, crippled.

Franklin wasn't indicted for that crime but further convictions soon followed in Mississippi and Ohio. In Missouri, he was given a death sentence for the murder of Gerald Gordon. He currently awaits execution for that crime.

Janie Lou Gibbs

Married at the tender age of 15, and a grandmother by the time she was 34, Janie Lou Gibbs was a soft-spoken, churchgoing woman from Cordele, Georgia. Fervent in her faith, Janie Lou taught Sunday school, served on numerous Church committees and ran a child care center for working mothers. When not so involved, she was devoted to her husband and three sons, for whom she enjoyed cooking hearty meals.

On January 21, 1966, tragedy struck the Gibbs family when Janie Lou's husband of 18 years, Charles Clayton Gibbs, died at the age of 39. Charles had shown no signs of being unwell, but doctors concluded that undiagnosed liver disease had caused his death. Janie Lou received a small insurance payout. She donated a portion to her church in gratitude for the support they'd given her.

In the wake of Charles Gibbs' death, the family pulled together but within a year they were struck by another tragedy. Janie's son

Marvin, aged just 13, collapsed in severe pain on August 29, 1966. He was rushed to hospital but died the same day. Again the church community gathered around Gibbs. Overwhelmed by their show of support, she again gave a portion of the life insurance payment to the church.

It would not be long before Janie Lou would call on the support of her congregation again. Just five months later, 16-year-old Melvin died, with similar symptoms to his father and brother. This time, doctors blamed hepatitis. The insurance company was not so convinced and called for an autopsy, which Janie refused on religious grounds. And so Melvin was buried and the grieving mother donated a portion of her insurance windfall to the work of God.

Among all of the tragedy, there was at least one happy event. Janie's oldest son, Roger, was married but still living at home. In August 1967, his wife bore him a son, making Janie Lou a grandmother.

The boy was named Ronnie Edward, and he was a healthy child until, at six weeks, his health inexplicably took a turn for the worse. He died soon after and although an autopsy was performed, it turned up nothing untoward. Then Roger himself became ill, showing the same frightening symptoms. Two days later he joined his father, siblings, and baby son in the grave.

By now, the spate of mysterious deaths had raised suspicions and despite Gibbs' protestations, an autopsy was performed, with tissue samples sent to the Georgia State Crime Laboratory. Two months later the results were in, showing large quantities of arsenic. An exhumation order was then obtained for other deceased members of the Gibbs family. They too were found to have died of arsenic poisoning.

Janie Gibbs was arrested, but a psychiatric evaluation found her to be suffering from schizophrenia and therefore unfit to stand trial. That diagnosis was revisited in 1976 when she was declared sane. She was subsequently sentenced to five consecutive life terms for the murders.

In April 1999, Gibbs was released on medical parole after she was found to be suffering from advanced Parkinson's disease. She died at a nursing home in Douglasville, Georgia on February 7, 2001, without ever revealing why she'd laced her family's meals with rat poison.

Bertha Gifford

Bertha Gifford was one of America's first recorded female serial killers, a death-obsessed "Good Samaritan," who served her local community as an unofficial nurse and was always ready to rush to the aid of an ailing neighbor, no matter what the hour or weather.

Gifford was born in Grubville, Missouri in 1872, one of ten children of William Poindexter Williams and his wife Matilda. In December 1894, she married Henry Graham and after his death, she married Eugene Gifford in 1907. The Giffords moved to rural Catawissa, in Franklin County, Missouri where Bertha acquired a reputation for her extraordinary cooking skills and for her caring nature.

This latter quality was best illustrated in her willingness to dash to the bedside of any sick or dying neighbor within 20 miles. Her white nurse's uniform was always at the ready, hanging over a chair, and she'd drive her old car through any sort of weather, even blizzards, usually arriving ahead of the country doctor.

Although not a trained nurse, Bertha understood symptoms and medicines and could take a patient's temperature and attend to their nourishment and comfort needs. She also never asked for payment, which made her a popular assistant to the local doctors.

However, there was a sinister side to Mrs. Gifford's good deeds. She was a deathbed and funeral junkie, somehow exhilarated by being in the vicinity of death and dying. And if the patient showed signs of improvement or recovery, Bertha was not above easing them on their way with a spot of arsenic.

Her favorite patients were children, who were more inclined to swallow any elixir she pushed their way and less likely to ask questions or report her activities. She'd arrive on the scene in a flurry of activity and quickly take control of the sickroom, impressing the family with her knowledge and competence. Early in the evening, she'd send the concerned mother off to bed with the assurance that everything was under control.

Of course, by the following morning, the young patient would have deteriorated significantly or would already be dead. Bertha would then call the doctor and console the grieving family with assurances that their loved one had gone gently and with the very best care available right to the bitter end. Nobody ever suspected Bertha. After all, she cried harder and longer than any of them.

Inevitably, though, the number of deaths under her care began to sound alarm bells. Then, when Ed Brinley died (the seventeenth death under Bertha's care) the authorities took notice and started asking questions.

Mrs. Gifford had a ready explanation for each one of the deaths, but when it was discovered that she had purchased a steady supply of arsenic-based rat poison, Bertha was placed under arrest and brought before a grand jury.

The evidence was damning, a chain of seventeen murders dating back to the death of her first husband, Henry Graham, and ending with the demise of her neighbor, Ed Brinley. Bertha had given him an "elixir" to cure a hangover.

Bertha was charged with murder but continued to protest her innocence until police chief Andrew McConnell caught her out with a clever interrogation technique. Noticing that Bertha appeared particularly annoyed at the suggestion that she had poisoned 3-year-old Beulah Mounds, McConnell pressed her about the incident. Eventually, Bertha snapped at him, "I did not give any arsenic to that Pounds child."

"To whom did you give it then?" the chief asked, at which Bertha allegedly admitted poisoning Ed Brinley and several others. The exhumation of Brinley's body showed that he had indeed died of arsenic poisoning.

After a three-day trial, Bertha Gifford was found not guilty by reason of insanity. She was committed to the Missouri State Hospital, a mental institution, where she remained until her death in 1951.

Kristen Gilbert

Kristen Gilbert was born on November 13, 1967, in Fall River, Massachusetts. As a child, she excelled at school. However, as she entered her teen years, friends and family began to notice some disturbing signs. She became a habitual liar and was prone to displays of neurotic behavior.

These negative traits notwithstanding, Kristen graduated from high school at age sixteen, thereafter attending Greenfield Community College and gaining certification as a registered nurse in 1988. Later that year, she married Glenn Gilbert. In 1989, she joined the staff of the Veterans Hospital in Northampton, Massachusetts, where she excelled. She was even featured in the magazine "VA Practitioner" in April 1990.

Yet, despite her early promise at her job, it had not escaped the attention of Gilbert's peers that there were an inordinately high number of deaths on her watch. No one suspected anything untoward, but Gilbert began to be jokingly referred to as the "Angel of Death."

Not everyone saw the humor in the situation, though. In 1996, three of Gilbert's colleagues raised concerns about the number of cardiac arrest deaths on the ward. They also reported that the supply of epinephrine, a drug that mimics the effects of adrenaline, was severely depleted.

Hospital administrators agreed that it warranted investigation. Before the inquiry could be initiated, though, a bomb threat was called in to the hospital. It was later determined that Kristen Gilbert had made the call herself.

Despite her crude attempt to derail the investigation, it went ahead. Gilbert found herself charged with killing three patients - Henry Hudon, 35, Kenneth Cutting, 41, and Edward Skwira, 69 - and attempting to kill two more, with lethal doses of epinephrine. A fourth murder, that of Stanley Jagodowski, 66, was later added to the rap sheet.

According to the evidence, Gilbert injected her victims with epinephrine, causing their hearts to race out of control. Autopsies on the four victims found high concentrations of the drug.

Why exactly Gilbert murdered her patients is unclear, although staff members at Northampton speculate that she wanted to draw attention to herself and her ability to deal with emergency situations. Specifically, they believe that she was trying to impress James Perrault, a VA police officer with whom she later had an affair. VA hospital rules require that hospital police are present at any medical emergency.

And there were many emergency situations when Kristen Gilbert was on duty. Most of the patients survived, but of the 63 that didn't, 37 died with Kristen Gilbert in attendance. Hospital administrators believe that she may have been responsible for at least 80 deaths and over 300 medical emergencies.

Kristen Gilbert was eventually convicted in federal court on March 14, 2001. Although Massachusetts does not have a death penalty statute, she was eligible for that sanction as her crimes were committed on federal property.

However, a sentence of death requires a unanimous verdict on the part of the jury and as that was not achieved, the judgment defaulted automatically to life in prison without the possibility of parole. An additional 20 years was added for the attempted murder convictions.

Gilbert initially appealed the decision but later withdrew her petition, aware that a guilty verdict on retrial would have allowed prosecutors to pursue the death penalty. She is currently incarcerated at a federal prison in Texas.

Billy Glaze

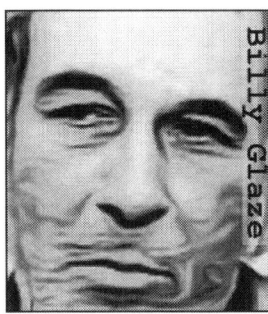

Billy Glaze (a.k.a. Jesse Sitting Crow) is a rarity in the annals of American crime, one of the few Native American serial killers on record. Arrested on August 31, 1987, while driving under the influence, Blaze was found to be in possession of a bloody shirt, plus a crowbar and nightstick with blood and hair stuck to them. This forensic evidence was later matched to three murder victims; Kathleen Bullman, Angeline Whitebird Sweet, and Angela Green.

The murders were committed over a ten-month period between July 1986 and April 1987. Each of the victims was a young Native American woman and the mother of young children. Each of them suffered from alcoholism and frequented the same taverns, bars where Glaze was also a regular.

Glaze's M.O. was startlingly similar in each case. He found his victims alone on the streets at night and bludgeoned them about the head and face. He then forced a stick into the victim's vagina and left her nude or semi-nude, posed in a degrading position.

Soon after the Angela Green murder on April 29, 1987, Minneapolis police were tipped off to Glaze as a potential suspect. Following up on this lead, they learned from Glaze's girlfriend, Lois Morrison, that Glaze had left the state and was living in New Mexico. Minnesota investigators then informed their New Mexico counterparts to be on the lookout for Glaze and he was arrested soon after on the DUI.

Back in Minnesota, Glaze voluntarily submitted hair, blood, and saliva samples for testing. The results of those tests led to him being charged with three counts of first-degree murder and three counts of sexual assault.

The forensic and eyewitness evidence presented at trial was overwhelming. Several witnesses testified that Glaze frequently made derogatory remarks about Native American women and spoke of his desire to sexually assault them with sticks, knives, and other objects. Witnesses also testified that Glaze had known each of the victims, and had been seen in the company of each woman shortly before she was killed.

Additionally, Glaze had given a pearl ring belonging to Angela Green to a friend of his. A print found at one of the crime scenes was also matched to a pair of sneakers he owned.

Perhaps most damning of all, a witness came forward to claim that he had actually seen Glaze kill Kathleen Bullman on July 27, 1987.

Another witness testified that he saw Glaze near the scene of Angela Green's murder on April 29, 1987.

With all of this evidence against him, Glaze began to crack. He allegedly confessed to a fellow inmate, saying he was afraid that he would be executed. Another inmate testified that Glaze told him: "I can't believe I killed them. I killed them with my hands."

On February 10, 1989, a jury convicted Glaze of three counts of first-degree murder. He was sentenced to three consecutive terms of life imprisonment and is currently serving his time in an out-of-state prison.

Since his incarceration, Glaze has continued to protest his innocence. The authorities don't believe him. In fact, he remains a suspect in the murders of at least 50 women in multiple states.

Billy Gohl

There were many stories about Billy Gohl doing the rounds in Aberdeen, Washington, many of them emanating from the man himself. Some said he'd once cannibalized a man in the Yukon, others that he'd been a pirate, still others that he'd bombed a cigar store and shot up boats manned by non-union sailors.

But no matter how many tall tales were attributed to him, there was one thing on which everyone agreed; Billy Gohl was a nasty piece of work, not the kind of man you'd want to meet in a dark alley, definitely not someone to be trifled with.

The short, bullnecked Billy, drifted into Aberdeen in the early 1900's, returning from the Yukon like so many speculators, broke and looking for work. This he found as a bartender in one of the tough waterfront saloons. Soon after, the bodies of deceased migrant workers started being fished out of the water in the vicinity of his saloon. If Gohl was suspected, the authorities never bothered questioning him.

In 1903, Billy Gohl moved on to more lucrative employment – he became a Sailor's Union official. The job was perfectly suited to a thug like Gohl. His fearsome reputation and intimidating physique were a natural deterrent to anyone contemplating strike action and he was also able to swell the union ranks with new members – few would be foolish enough to decline an "invitation" from Gohl.

After Gohl became head of the Union office in 1909, he spied an enticing opportunity for enriching himself. His method was simplicity itself. Sailors arriving in town would typically call on the union offices to pick up mail, check for any ships recruiting crew, and stash any valuables before hitting the town for a night of drinking and debauchery.

Gohl would be at the Union office himself, ready to greet them. If the man was alone, Gohl would ask whether he had family or friends in the area. If he was just passing through and therefore unlikely to be missed, and if he was carrying anything vaguely of value, Gohl would then lock the front door so they would not be disturbed. Then he'd shoot, stab, beat, or strangle the man to death, relieve him of his valuables, and discard the body through a specially designed chute he had installed in the floor.

So productive was Gohl in these activities that between 1909 and 1912, Aberdeen became known as the port from whence sailors did not return. And if he was responsible for even half of the murder victims pulled from the water, Billy Gohl ranks as

America's most prolific serial killer ever. In the period from 1909 to 1913, the waters around Aberdeen yielded some 200 corpses, most of them believed to be sailors.

Perhaps to deflect attention, Gohl was extremely outspoken in his criticism of police efforts to apprehend the killer. He berated them at every opportunity, demanding that they solve the murders and provide greater protection for his union members. He insisted that they apprehend the man or men responsible and unfortunately for Gohl they eventually did, although in truth, he was primarily the architect of his own downfall.

After dispatching his latest victim, Gohl plundered the corpse and came across a pocket watch with the name August Schleuter engraved on it. The watch was attractive, but Gohl knew that it could easily be traced to the victim, so he returned it to the man's pocket before dumping him in the drink.

A few days later, the corpse washed up on shore and Gohl was called to identify the body. "Yes," he said immediately, "That's August Schleuter. He came in a few days ago to check his mail." Unfortunately, for Gohl, the man's name was actually Fred Nielsen, and the engraving on the watch was the name of the watchmaker. How though, could Gohl have known the name unless he himself had killed Nielsen?

Gohl was convicted of murder in 1913. The death penalty in Washington having been repealed the previous year, he was spared the noose and sentenced instead to life in prison. He died there, 14 years later.

David Alan Gore

Killer cousins David Gore and Fred Waterfield loved two things, guns and women. The former they indulged with hunting and, in Gore's case, taking a course in gunsmithing, the latter they fed by unleashing a three-year reign of terror on the women of Florida from 1981 to 1983.

It was 1976 when the cousins first hit on the idea of stalking and raping women. Their early efforts met with varied success. Several potential victims escaped, as much due to the cousins' ineptitude as to anything else. When they eventually succeeded in their first rape, they were promptly arrested, although the victim later refused to testify and they were released.

By early 1981, Gore was working as caretaker of a citrus grove, and patrolling the streets at night, as an auxiliary sheriff's deputy.

Waterfield had moved to Orlando, but he still visited Gore regularly in Vero Beach. It was during one of these visits that Waterfield suggested that they resume their "hunts." Gore, after all, was in the perfect situation – the Sheriff's badge would allow him to easily gain control of potential victims, while any bodies could be buried in the vast orchards. So enthused was Waterfield by the idea, that he offered Gore $1,000 for any pretty girl he managed to abduct.

On February 19, 1981, Gore spotted 17-year-old Ying Hua Ling and tricked her into his car, using his police badge. He then drove her home, where he also took her mother into custody. With the two women securely handcuffed, he phoned Waterfield, then drove to the orchard. While he waited for Waterfield, Gore raped both of the women. Then, when Waterfield eventually arrived, he too raped Ying Hua, before strangling her. Mrs. Ling meanwhile had been bound with a rope around her neck and in her efforts to escape had choked to death. Waterfield departed the scene, leaving Gore to dispose of the bodies. Gore got $400 for his trouble.

Five months later, on July 15, Gore abducted 35-year-old Judith Daley from Round Island Park. Waterfield was happy that Gore had delivered the blonde he had requested and paid $1,500 for the pleasure of raping her. Gore was again left to dispose of the corpse and would later testify that he'd "fed her to the alligators," in a swamp west of Interstate 95.

A week later, a local man reported Gore for trying to force his teenaged daughter into a vehicle. Gore was stripped of his badge and was soon in even deeper trouble. He was arrested while hiding in a woman's car, armed with a pistol and a pair of handcuffs. That offense drew a 5-year prison term, but Gore served less than two, before being paroled.

A short while later, Waterfield moved back to Vero Beach, and their deadly hunts resumed. On May 21, they abducted, raped, and killed, two 14-year-olds, Angelica Lavallee and Barbara Byer.

Then, on July 26, 1983, Vero Beach authorities received a report of a man firing shots at a naked girl on a residential street. Officers rushed to the scene and found a car with blood dripping from its trunk. Inside, the body of 17-year-old Lynn Elliott lay with a bullet lodged in her skull. Confronted by the police, Gore meekly surrendered, and a search of the house turned up a naked 14-year-old girl tied to the rafters in the attic.

The surviving victim told police that she and Elliott had been hitchhiking when Gore and another man picked them up, threatened them with a gun, then brought them to the house where they were stripped, tied up and raped repeatedly. Elliott managed to escape, but Gore chased after her and shot her in the street.

Under interrogation, Gore quickly cracked and confessed to the crimes he and his cousin had committed. On March 16, 1984, he was sentenced to death for the murder of Lynn Elliott.

Waterfield went on trial for the Byer/Levallee murders on January 21, 1985. He was sentenced to two life terms without parole for at least 50 years.

David Gore was executed by lethal injection on April 12, 2012.

Dana Sue Gray

On March 10, 1994, 57-year-old Dorinda Hawkins was tending the antiques store where she worked in Lake Elsinore, California, when a petite, blonde woman walked in. The woman said she wanted to browse for picture frames, so Hawkins let her and then went back to her work.

The customer continued browsing, at one point asking Hawkins if she was working in the store alone. Then, while Hawkins' back was turned, she suddenly felt something looped around her throat and pressure being applied. To her horror, she realized that she was being strangled.

Hawkins was not about to give up without a fight. For several minutes, she alternately struggled and pleaded with her attacker. Eventually, she found herself blacking out. She woke some forty minutes later to the sound of a phone ringing. Staggering to her feet she was able to call an ambulance, which soon arrived to rush her to hospital. There, Dorinda was able to give police a description of her attacker – about 5-foot-two, mid-thirties, with a slim build and longish blond hair. Little did Dorinda know that she'd just survived the attentions of a female serial killer, who had already claimed at least two other victims.

Norma Davis, an active 87-year-old, had been found strangled, stabbed and battered to death on February 14, 1994. Although her home was in a quiet, gated community, someone had gotten to her, leaving her with two butcher's knives protruding from her neck. She'd been stabbed 11 times, the lacerations to her throat so severe that she was almost decapitated.

On February 28, the killer struck again, killing another Canyon Lake resident. Friends of June Roberts were concerned when she didn't pick up the phone to receive their good wishes on her 66th birthday. When they called on her home on Big Tee Drive, they found the elderly woman strangled with a telephone cord and bludgeoned to death with a wine bottle.

The police were baffled by the murders. Neither woman had been raped and robbery did not appear to be a motive as neither residence had been ransacked. The violence of the attacks suggested a personal motive, but friends and family were unable to suggest anyone who might have held a grudge against either of the victims. Then, with the attack on Dorinda Hawkins, the police began to suspect that there might be a link to the unknown blonde assailant.

A composite drawing was released to the media. However, although this looked like a solid lead, it would take another tragic death before the suspect was eventually apprehended.

On March 16, 1994, Dora Beebe, another 87-year-old, was attacked and killed in her home. Even, by the standards of the previous murders, this one was particularly brutal. The elderly lady had been battered to death with an iron, the attack so vicious that when the body was removed to the morgue, the victim's shape could still be seen on the floor, outlined in blood.

A break in the case came when police learned that both June Roberts' and Norma Davis' credit cards had been used after their deaths. In fact, the cards had been used on the very days the murders were committed and wherever had used them had gone on a shopping spree, charging beauty treatments, perfumes, expensive clothes and shoes, jewelry, gourmet food, even toys. The woman who had used the cards bore a strong resemblance to the attacker in the Hawkins' assault and before long the police had made an arrest.

At 5-foot-two, slim and attractive, Dana Sue Gray made an unlikely serial killer. Still, the evidence recovered from her home, including June Roberts' bankbook and several items Gray had bought with the dead women's credit cards, was overwhelming.

Under interrogation, while not directly admitting to murder, Gray made several admissions and offered a most unusual motive. "I got desperate to buy things. Shopping puts me at rest. I'm lost without it."

Dana Sue Gray went on trial for murder on March 10, 1995. She initially entered an insanity plea, but faced with the prospect of execution, she changed her plea to guilty of the murders of June Roberts and Dora Beebe. No charges were brought in the Davis murder due to lack of evidence. Gray is also suspected of three other murders, in Riverside and San Diego.

On October 16, 1998, Dana Sue Gray was sentenced to life in prison without parole. She is incarcerated at the California Women's Prison in Chowchilla.

James Waybern Hall

On March 14, 1944, James Waybern Hall, recently dishonorably ejected from the U.S. Navy, married 19-year-old Fayrene Clemmons in Little Rock, Arkansas. The marriage was a stormy one, resulting in a brief separation within weeks of the nuptials. Then, on September 28, Hall paid a visit to his father-in-law to announce mournfully that Fayrene had deserted him three days earlier.

The police were called and listened sympathetically to the dejected husband's tale of his bride's promiscuous behavior. Within a week they'd closed their case, declaring that Fayrene had probably run off with another man. This theory appeared to be vindicated when relatives received a Christmas card from Fayrene, postmarked Bakersfield, California. The police were keen to examine the card, but before they could, James Hall asked to borrow the card and envelope and then reported that he'd lost them.

On January 29, 1945, loggers in Ouachita County, southwest of Little Rock, discovered an abandoned car. Slumped over the steering wheel, with a bullet wound to the heart, was a man, later identified as Carl Hamilton, a barber from Camden. He'd been dead several days and the police speculated that he'd been a victim of a robbery. They certainly had no reason to link his death to the disappearance of a wayward spouse in Little Rock.

Another murder occurred on February 1. This time, E.C. Adams vanished on his way to his job at a war industry plant in Little Rock. His car was later found outside of Fordyce, in Dallas County. Police searched the immediate area and found Adams' body hidden in nearby brush with a single bullet lodged in the brain. That same day, a trucker named Doyle Mulherin went missing while making a routine delivery. His truck turned up near Stuttgart, some 40 miles southeast of Little Rock. Doyle was found nearby, a bullet wound to the head. $125 in company cash had been stolen from the truck.

On March 2, James Hall was arrested for his involvement in a Little Rock bar fight. Found guilty of simple assault, he avoided jail time by paying a fine. However, during the course of their investigation, the police found out some interesting information about Hall. They learned, for example, that on January 28, he'd borrowed a car from a friend. There was a loaded pistol in the glove compartment, and when the car was returned, the owner discovered that a single round had been fired from it. The weapon was surrendered to police for testing and ballistics proved that it was the weapon used to kill Carl Hamilton.

On March 9, 1945, a burned-out car was found near Heber Springs, in Cleburne County. On the backseat, police found the incinerated body of J.D. Newcomb, Jr., late of Little Rock.

Police had meanwhile obtained a warrant for James Hall's lodgings, where they found a large quantity of ammunition as well as equipment stolen from Carl Hamilton.

Confronted with the evidence, Hall immediately confessed to the murders of Hamilton, Adams, Mulherin, and Newcomb. The motive had been robbery, he said, but the murders had netted him less than $300 overall. He also led police to the skeletal remains of his wife. Fayrene was identified by her crooked teeth.

Hall's trial in May 1945 lasted just two days and resulted in a guilty verdict and a sentence of death. Unlike many convicted murderers, he went laughing and joking to the chair. "Boys, I'm not afraid," he told the guards as they strapped him in. "I can take it."

Charles Ray Hatcher

Charles Ray Hatcher was born on July 16, 1929, in Mound City, Missouri, the youngest of four children. His father was an ex-con and an abusive alcoholic who doled out regular beatings to his kids. Hatcher endured a difficult childhood. When he was just 6 years old, his brother was accidentally electrocuted right before his eyes. His parents divorced soon after and his mother remarried several times, landing the boy with a succession of abusive stepfathers.

Hatcher's first brush with the law came in 1947, when he was convicted of stealing a truck from his employer and received a two-year suspended sentence. Undeterred by this setback, he fell into a life of petty crime and served time variously for auto theft, forgery, and burglary. By 1959, the 30-year-old Hatcher had already served six prison terms. Soon though, he'd graduate from petty crimes against property to violent offenses against people.

On June 26, 1959, Hatcher was arrested after attempting to abduct a 16-year-old boy at knifepoint. Sent down for five years, Hatcher was returned to the Missouri State Penitentiary, where he boasted that he was the state's most notorious criminal since Jesse James.

On July 2, 1961, inmate Jerry Tharrington was found raped and stabbed to death in the prison kitchen. Hatcher was suspected of the murder but there wasn't enough evidence to convict him. Instead, he spent time in solitary confinement before being returned to the general prison population. He remained there until August 24, 1963.

After his release, Hatcher drifted for a while, eventually ending up in California. On August 27, 1969, he abducted twelve-year-old William Freeman in Antioch, California, took him to a creek, then sexually molested and strangled him. Two days later, he abducted six-year-old Gilbert Martinez in San Francisco. Hatcher was arrested in the act of beating and sexually assaulting the boy.

Facing another extended prison term for the crime, Hatcher claimed insanity, alleging that he heard voices. There followed an extended round of psychiatric evaluations, some doctors declaring him unfit to stand trial, others convinced that he was exaggerating his symptoms.

Eventually, on May 24, 1971, Hatcher was sent to trial and pleaded not guilty by reason of insanity. A new round of evaluations followed, during which time Hatcher escaped from the hospital and went on the run. Captured a week later, he was declared unfit to stand trial and sent to the prison hospital at Vacaville.

It was only in August 1972, that Hatcher finally faced the music for the abduction and attempted rape of Gilbert Martinez. In December 1972, he was found guilty and sent to the California State Hospital as a mentally disordered sexual offender.

In June 1976, the California Parole Board declared that Hatcher's condition had improved dramatically and in May 1977 he was released to a halfway house.

On May 26, 1978, four-year-old Eric Christgen disappeared in downtown Saint Joseph, Missouri. His body was later found along the Missouri River. He had been sexually abused and then strangled.

The police focused their investigation on Melvin Reynolds, a mentally retarded 25-year-old and, despite a lack of evidence, they eventually coaxed a confession out of him. Reynolds was tried and sentenced to life in prison, while the real killer, Charles Hatcher, was free to kill again.

On July 29, 1983, hikers found the nude, battered body of 11-year-old Michelle Steele on the banks of the Missouri River near St. Joseph. She had been raped, strangled and beaten to death. Arrested for the murder the following day, Hatcher broke down and started confessing. He claimed to have killed 15 other children between 1969 and 1983, the murders traversing California, Iowa, Missouri, and Illinois.

Among his other victims, he named James Churchill of Davenport Iowa, and drew investigators a map, which allowed them to recover the boy's body. He also confessed to killing Eric Christgen, a crime for which Melvin Reynolds had already served four years.

Hatcher was convicted of the Christgen murder in October 1983, and sentenced to life imprisonment with no parole for at least 50 years. A year later, he went on trial for killing Michelle Steele. Hatcher asked for the death penalty but the jury opted for life imprisonment. It was a term Charles Hatcher would never serve. On December 3, 1984, he hanged himself in his cell at the state prison in Jefferson City.

Dale Hausner

For a period of 14 months, from May 2005 to July 2006, the city of Phoenix, Arizona, was terrorized by a deadly serial shooter. The killer struck at random, targeting pedestrians, cyclists, and animals in a series of drive-by shootings. By the time police officers eventually closed in to arrest Dale Hausner and his sometime accomplice Samuel Dieteman, six people lay dead, 19 others had been injured and the shooter had also shot seven dogs and three horses.

The serial shooter first came to public attention on June 29, when 20-year-old David Estrada was shot dead on a Tolleson street. That same night, a horse was shot in a nearby field and over the next five months, the killer turned his attention to animals, shooting another horse and three dogs, killing one of them. Then, on November 11, he claimed another human victim, Nathaniel Shoffner, shot and killed as he stood on a sidewalk near his home.

After the Shoffner murder, the killer laid low for a period of six weeks. Then, on December 29, he was back with a vengeance, claiming two victims in a single night, wounding another and shooting a dog. The following night he struck again, wounding a female pedestrian and shooting three dogs, one of them fatally.

By now, the police were certain that they were dealing with a serial killer, but despite their investigative efforts and a $5,000 reward for information, the murderer remained at large.

On May 6, he reappeared in Scottsdale, wounding a pedestrian and fatally shooting 20-year-old Claudia Gutierrez-Cruz.

This latest murder seemed to spur him on. There were 14 shooting incidents and a stabbing over the next three months. None of these were fatal, but the killer did claim a final victim. 22-year-old Robin Blasnek was shot and killed at approximately 11:15 p.m. on July 30, as she walked to her boyfriend's house.

Yet even after six murders and numerous other attacks, the police had no leads on the man they were chasing. What they did know was that he attacked from a vehicle using a small caliber weapon or a shotgun. The attacks were all carried out at night or in the early morning hours. Where animals were shot, they were being kept behind chain-link fencing on corner lots.

It didn't amount to much and police might have had a hard time solving the murders if Dale Hausner had been able to keep his mouth shut. Instead, the 33-year-old father of three bragged to a friend, Ron Horton, about the murders and Horton went to the cops.

After a four-day surveillance, Hausner and his roommate, Samuel Dieteman, were taken into custody. A search of Hausner's home turned up firearms, newspaper clippings about the murders, and a map of the Phoenix area with red dots marking the sites of the attacks.

Initially, Hausner denied any knowledge of the shootings, but after Dieteman turned state's evidence, Hausner confessed. He went on trial on March 23, 2009, charged with 8 murders, 19 attempted murders, numerous aggravated assaults, firearms charges, cruelty to animals, and arson. Dieteman was charged with (and pled guilty to) two murders, plus conspiracy to commit murder.

On March 27, 2009, Dale Hausner was sentenced to six death penalties. He currently awaits execution on Arizona's death row.

J. Frank Hickey

In the early years of the 20th century, a trio of sensational child murder cases captured the public attention in America. The first was the case of the notorious "Werewolf of Wisteria," Albert Fish, a depraved sadist and cannibal who killed and consumed an undetermined number of children; the second was Peter Kudzinowski, a Polish immigrant electrocuted for the sex murders of three children; the third, and least known of the three, was John Frank Hickey, the so-called "Postcard Killer."

On October 11, 1911, a 7-year-old named Joey Joseph disappeared from the streets of Lackawanna, New York. His father immediately reported the disappearance to the police but despite an intensive search, they were unable to find any trace of him. It was as though the boy had vanished into thin air.

Shortly after the disappearance, a letter arrived at the Joseph residence describing how Joey had been killed. It was followed by a number of other letters and postcards, addressed both to the boy's parents and to the police. The writer claimed to be Joey's killer and expressed remorse for the boy's death, but it was clear what he was doing. Serial killers often get off on reliving their crimes. He was doing this by taunting the grieving family.

Eventually, a letter arrived giving directions to the boy's body and the next day the police dug up Joey's skeletal remains from beneath a communal outhouse. The discovery caused a media sensation, placing pressure on the police to apprehend the killer.

With no leads to go on, the authorities decided to publish the postcards in a local newspaper. It was a long shot, but almost immediately several people came forward, claiming that they recognized the handwriting. Most of them pointed the finger at J. Frank Hickey, known locally as a somewhat eccentric drunk.

Hickey was arrested and soon confessed to killing Joey, as well as a 10-year-old newspaper boy named Michael Kruck and a 34-year-old man named Edwin W. Morey. In addition, Hickey confessed to numerous sexual assaults, confiding to officers that he was sexually attracted to children. When drunk, he said, he was unable to control his compulsion and the attacks had occurred under these circumstances.

Hickey was placed on trial for murder but, unusual for the era, he escaped the electric chair and was convicted only of second-degree murder. He was sent to Auburn prison where he remained until his death.

But how many murders did Hickey actually commit? Given his self-described compulsion and the time elapsed between his first murder and his eventual conviction almost three decades later, it is almost certainly more than the three he admitted to.

Hickey was, in fact, suspected of at least twelve murders. During the decades that he roamed New England, dozens of children went missing or were found murdered. At least some of these fell victim to serial killers (such as Fish and Kudzinowski, described earlier) and some were almost certainly killed by J. Frank Hickey.

Johann Otto Hoch

Johann Otto Hoch, who would later achieve infamy as the "Stockyard Bluebeard," was born Johann Schmidt in 1855, at Horweiler, Germany. In the 1890's, he immigrated to the United States where he dropped his birth name and adopted assorted pseudonyms under which he married and swindled a succession of women, at least 55 of them, between 1890 and 1905. If the victim was lucky, she'd find herself relieved of her money and abandoned. However, in at least 15 cases, Hoch's brides were sent to an agonizing death with arsenic.

Hoch's first (and only legal) wife was Christine Ramb, with whom he had three children before he deserted her in 1887. By 1895, he'd married and abandoned at least eight women, some of whom had allegedly died. In February of that year, he showed up in Wheeling, West Virginia, using the name Jacob Huff. He soon won the heart of a middle-aged widow named Caroline Hoch, marrying her in April.

Three months later, Caroline fell gravely ill. The local vicar was called to her bedside where, according to his later testimony, he saw "Huff" give her an elixir. She died in agony three days later, whereupon "Huff" cleaned out her bank account, sold her house, and collected $2,500 in life insurance benefits. He then vanished, leaving his clothes, his watch, and a note on the bank of the Ohio River. Suicide was suspected, but no body was ever found.

Hoch, of course, was not dead. Using his latest victim's surname (a macabre practice he adopted throughout his criminal career) he moved to Chicago, where he found work in the meatpacking plants.

While in Chicago, Hoch was sentenced to a year in jail for defrauding a used-furniture dealer. The arresting officer, Inspector George Shippy, also suspected Hoch of bigamy and began looking into his background. He soon found evidence of dozens of missing or deserted women, from New York City to San Francisco and all points in between. But solid evidence proved elusive until Shippy learned of the death of Caroline Hoch in Wheeling. An autopsy was ordered, but the body was found to be gutted, all vital organs removed.

Hoch meanwhile had been released from prison and had left Chicago. Over the next ten years, he married at least another 15 women. Except now, his modus operandi had changed. Aware that the police were tracking his movements, Hoch began killed more swiftly.

On December 5, 1904, he married Marie Walcker in Chicago, killing her within days of the wedding. On the night of Marie's death, Hoch proposed to her sister, Amelia. They were married within six days of the hastily arranged funeral, whereupon Hoch promptly disappeared with $750 of his new bride's money.

The police were summoned and an exhumation and autopsy were ordered on Marie Walcker. It turned up copious amounts of arsenic.

With evidence of murder finally obtained, Hoch's picture was sent to every major newspaper in America. In New York City, a middle-aged landlady recognized Hoch as "Henry Bartels," a new tenant who had proposed to her within 20 minutes of renting a room. She called the police and Hoch was arrested.

Otto Hoch went on trial charged with Marie Walcker's murder. When he was eventually found guilty and sentenced to hang, he responded by telling the court: "It's all over with Johann. It serves me right." He went to the gallows on February 23, 1906.

Anthony Kirkland

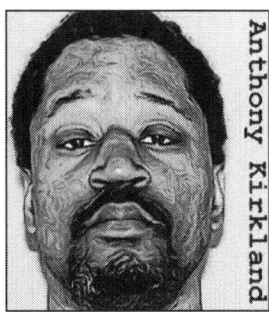

Anthony Kirkland had done this before. In March 1987, aged just 18, Kirkland had choked and beaten his 28-year-old girlfriend, Leola Douglas, during an argument at his Walnut Hills home. Not content with that, he'd doused the woman in lighter fluid and set her on fire, killing her. Arrested for that murder he copped a plea to voluntary manslaughter and drew a 16-year prison term.

Now, barely five and a half years after his release, he stood accused of four brutal rape-murders and this time the prosecutor was determined that Anthony Kirkland would get the death penalty.

Kirkland had been released on September 3, 2003, his period of parole supervision expiring on October 25, 2004. Three months later he was in trouble again, this time for the knifepoint rape of a female neighbor. Acquitted on that charge, Kirkland determined that no victim would ever live to testify against him again.

On May 11, 2006, the burned body of 14-year-old Casonya Crawford was found just off Blair Avenue in Avondale, Cincinnati. Kirkland was suspected, but there was no concrete evidence against him. Then, on June 16, the burned corpse of 45-year-old Mary Jo Newton was discovered. And another burned body turned up on December 22, that of 14-year-old Kimya Rolison. Kirkland was again a suspect, but again the fire had obliterated any usable forensic evidence.

On May 14, 2007, a SWAT team was dispatched to Kirkland's home to deal with a domestic violence incident. Kirkland was found to be holding his 18-month-old son hostage, and threatening to kill the boy. He was sentenced to 115 days in jail for the incident.

No sooner had he been released than he was again under arrest, this time for soliciting sex from his girlfriend's 13-year-old daughter. The sentence of the court was a year in prison, while he was also required to register as a sex offender.

Released in October 2008, Kirkland entered the Pogue Rehabilitation Center, a halfway house in Over-the-Rhine. He was evicted soon after, for fighting with other residents.

On March 1, 2009, Kirkland broke into the home of Frederick Hughes. He attacked Hughes with a pair of scissors, inflicting at least 10 stab wounds. Hughes survived the attack and his description of the assailant led to an arrest warrant being issued against Kirkland for burglary and felonious assault.

But where was Kirkland?

On March 5, he showed up at the home of Roberta Baldwin, the mother of his child, and threatened her with a knife. Three days later, on March 8, 13-year-old Esme Kenney went missing while jogging near her home in Winton Hills. A search team was dispatched and found Kirkland sleeping against a tree in nearby woods. In his possession, officers found Esme's watch and iPod, although Kirkland denied any knowledge of her whereabouts.

Esme's body was found three hours later, hidden in brush just 100 yards from where Kirkland had been sleeping. She'd been strangled and the lower part of her body had been burned, apparently in an attempt to hide evidence of sexual assault. Kirkland was then arrested and charged with murder.

Anthony Kirkland went on trial in August 2009. He pled not guilty but was convicted on 12 counts, including first-degree murder. He was sentenced to death and currently awaits execution on Ohio's death row.

Adam Leroy Lane

On the evening of July 30, 2007, 16-year-old Shea McDonough returned to her home in Chelmsford, Massachusetts after visiting friends. Arriving just before midnight, Shea left the back door unlocked thinking that her brother would be home soon afterwards. Her parents, Kevin and Jeannie, were already asleep, so Shea went straight to bed.

A short while later, Jeannie McDonough was awakened by muffled moans coming from her daughter's bedroom. She roused her husband. Sensing that something was not right, the couple immediately went to Shea's room.

The sight that greeted them initially confused Jeannie. For a brief moment, she thought that their son was playing a prank on them. Then the cold realization hit home. There was a man in the room, a big, burly man dressed all in black and wearing a mask. He was leaning over Shea. He had a large hunting knife to her throat.

Kevin and Jeannie sprung immediately into action, tackling the much larger man and eventually subduing him in a ferocious struggle. Jeannie's hands were severely lacerated during the fight. She said later that she barely felt the razor-sharp blade slice through her fingers as she wrested the knife from the attacker.

"We did what any other parent would have done in the same situation, protect your child and go into survival mode," she later said.

With the man subdued, Shea called the police, who were soon on the scene to take the assailant into custody. He was identified as Adam Leroy Lane, a long-haul trucker, married with three daughters. As the police searched his truck they turned up a collection of knives, as well as a choke wire and a DVD entitled "Hunting Humans." The police did not know it yet, but they'd just arrested a serial killer.

Lane was soon connected, via DNA found on one of his knives, to a brutal murder that had occurred just 22 hours before his attack on Shea McDonough. As in the McDonough case, Lane entered through an unlocked door and attacked Monica Massaro in her New Jersey home. Massaro's throat was viciously slashed before Lane inflicted multiple stab wounds to her body.

Lane initially denied any involvement in the murder. However, he eventually broke down and confessed, although he was adamant that the attack was not sexually motivated. "I love my wife very much," he insisted.

Another charge soon followed. On the night of July 13, 2007, mother of two Darlene Ewalt had stayed up late on the patio and was talking to a friend on the phone after her husband had gone to bed. Darlene's friend heard a muffled sound on the line and then the phone went dead. Concerned, she got her husband to drive her to Darlene's house where they discovered the woman's battered body lying on the patio. Darlene's husband and son were initially arrested for the crime, but DNA evidence would eventually point the finger at the real murderer - Adam Lane.

Just three days after the Ewalt murder, Lane attacked Patricia Brooks in York County, Pennsylvania. Brooks survived but suffered severe injuries.

Adam Lane was sentenced to 25 years for the attack on Shea McDonough. He received 10-20 years for the attack of Patricia Brooks. For the murder of Monica Massaro, he was sentenced to 50 years. Faced with a possible death sentence for killing Darlene Ewalt, Lane entered a plea agreement and accepted a sentence of 48 years to life. He remains a suspect in two more murders and another non-fatal knife attack.

James Marlow & Cynthia Coffman

There is little in Cynthia Coffman's past to suggest the murderess she would become. The pampered daughter of a wealthy St. Louis businessman, she was raised in a devout Catholic home.

As a Catholic, abortion was, of course, unthinkable, so when Cynthia got pregnant at age 17, her parents insisted that she marry the father of her child. Five years in a loveless marriage and Cynthia had had enough. Leaving her child behind, she got into her car and headed west with little more than the clothes on her back. She landed in Page, Arizona, where she got a job waiting tables and shacked up with a local man. Eventually, they were evicted after numerous complaints about their drunken all-night parties.

On May 8, 1986, Cynthia and her boyfriend were pulled over after running a stop sign in Barstow, California. A search of their vehicle produced an unlicensed pistol and a quantity of methamphetamine and the couple was arrested. Cynthia avoided jail time, but her boyfriend drew six weeks in the county jail, and it was while visiting him there that Cynthia met his cellmate, James Marlow.

Marlow was a career criminal, currently doing time for theft. Before that, he'd served three years at Folsom for a series of home invasion robberies. He had been known during that stretch as "The Folsom Wolf," and he proudly wore the tattoos of the neo-Nazi Aryan Brotherhood.

It was love at first sight and, once Marlow was released, Coffman forgot her former lover and headed with Marlow to Arizona, where he had family. But Marlow's relatives soon tired of their sponging and before long the couple found that they'd worn out their welcome. Eventually, they were reduced to sleeping in the woods and to raising funds the only way they knew how.

On July 26, 1986, Coffman and Marlow burglarized a home in Whitley County, Kentucky, making off with cash, jewelry, and a shotgun.

A few days after that burglary, the couple was married in Tennessee. Cynthia celebrated the occasion by having the legend: "I belong to the Folsom Wolf," tattooed across her butt.

They headed west again, arriving in Costa Mesa, California, in early October.

On the evening of October 11, 1986, 32-year-old Sandra Neary failed to return home after driving to an automatic teller machine to withdraw cash. Police later found her car abandoned in a parking lot. Two weeks passed before her decomposing remains were found by hikers near Corona, in Riverside County.

Less than three weeks later, on October 28, Pamela Simmons, 35, went missing from Bullhead City, Arizona. Police theorized that she had been snatched while drawing cash from a curbside ATM.

Then, on November 7, 20-year-old Corinna Novis vanished from a shopping mall in Redlands, California. And on November 12, 19-year-old psychology student Lynel Murray failed to show up for a date with her boyfriend. Lynel's car was found parked outside the dry cleaning shop where she worked. The following day, her naked, strangled corpse was discovered in a Huntington Beach motel room. There was evidence that she had been raped.

Not long after, police had their first break in the case, when Corinna Novis' checkbook was found in a dumpster in Laguna Niguel. It was stashed inside a takeout bag that also contained papers bearing the names, Cynthia Coffman and James Marlow. Using this information, investigators tracked Marlow and Coffman to a San Bernardino motel room, where they found sheets of paper on which the couple had practiced Lynel Murray's signature. A statewide alert was then issued for both fugitives.

On November 14, 1986, officers were summoned to a lodge at Big Bear City, California, where the manager had recognized two of his guests as the fugitives. Their room was empty, but a search of the nearby woods uncovered the suspects, hiking along a mountain road. They surrendered without a fight, and within hours Coffman had led officers to a vineyard near Fontana, where Corinna Novis was found, buried in a shallow grave. She'd been raped, sodomized and strangled.

Marlow and Coffman stood trial for murder in July 1989 and were both sentenced to death, making Cynthia Coffman the first woman to received the death penalty in California since its reinstatement.

Lee Roy Martin

Ann Dedmond could be argumentative when she'd been drinking and those arguments often ended with her getting into her car and driving off. So when exactly that happened on March 1, 1967, Ann's husband, Roger, was unconcerned. He knew that she'd be back once she'd cooled down.

Except this time Ann didn't return. The following morning Roger got a call to say that Ann had been found dead in the center of the highway between the towns of Union, South Carolina, and Spindale, North Carolina. He'd barely digested that shocking piece of news when he found himself the key suspect in her murder. Tried and found guilty, he was sentenced to 18 years and sent to Union County Prison Camp.

Two months later, on February 8, 1968, Bill Gibbons, editor of the local newspaper, The Gaffney Ledger, received a phone call. The caller claimed to be the killer of Ann Dedmond and also gave Gibbons detailed instructions to where two bodies could be found. Gibbons was unconvinced but passed the information on to the police anyway.

Following the instructions, officers traveled to an area near People's Creek Bridge where they found the body of 20-year-old Nancy Parris, reported missing by her husband the previous day. A second body was soon discovered, that of 14-year-old Nancy Rhinehart, missing for ten days. Both victims had been strangled and their bodies bore clear signs of torture, with numerous cigarette burns. It was speculated that Rhinehart had been held captive for 10 days before being killed.

On February 12, 1968, Bill Gibbons got another call from the self-confessed killer. He again claimed to have killed Ann Dedmond and threatened, "If they don't catch me, there will be more deaths."

He was good to his word. The following day, February 13, 15-year-old Opal Buckson was walking to get the bus to school. Her two younger siblings were lagging some 50 yards behind when they saw a man grab Opal and force her into the trunk of a blue Sedan. Opal's brother immediately raced home to call his father, but by the time Emanuel Buckson reached the scene, the blue Sedan was gone and the only sign of Opal was her school books scattered across the blacktop.

A massive search was launched for the missing girl. On February 15, two days since the abduction, civilian volunteers Theodore Lang and Frank Henders were searching along a rural road when they saw a man standing beside a blue sedan. On seeing them, the man quickly jumped into his car and drove off, but not before Henders jotted down his license plate number. They passed the information on to the police who concentrated their search efforts near the scene. They soon turned up Opal's body. Unlike the other victims, she'd been stabbed, but her body bore the now-familiar cigarette burns.

Investigators, meanwhile, had traced the plate number to a 30-year-old man named Lee Roy Martin. Martin was placed under surveillance while the police built up their case against him. He was arrested at work two days later and soon confessed to the killings.

Convicted of the four murders in 1969, Martin was sentenced to four life terms. He'd serve less than three years. On May 31, 1972, inmate Kenneth Rumsey stabbed Martin to death in a dispute over the affections of another prisoner.

Roger Dedmond was released in 1969, after serving a year in prison.

David Mason

From an early age, it was evident that something was not entirely right with David Mason. The son of strict Pentecostal parents, Mason displayed uncontrollably violent tendencies, even in childhood. He was a fire starter who indulged in self-mutilation and routinely attacked other children, including his own baby brother whom he once threatened with a knife. His parents responded with harsh punishments, beating him, locking him in his room, and subjecting him to verbal and psychological abuse. These treatments only served to make the problem worse and eventually they gave up. At age 14, David Mason was made a ward of the state.

After dropping out of school in the 9th grade, Mason hit the streets and was soon involved in a life of violent crime. In July 1977, he stabbed a clerk with an ice pick while robbing a store. That crime earned him 36 months in state prison.

Mason was a troublesome prisoner, racking up a number of offenses, including assaulting other prisoners, flooding a cellblock, and possession of contraband. Nonetheless, he was released in 1980, with tragic consequences for four elderly California residents.

Mason's first victim was a 73-year-old woman whom he'd known for several years. She had employed him for various odd jobs and had even invited him into her apartment, where she'd shown him her alarm system. Using this information to his advantage, Mason entered the residence on March 6, tied the victim up, robbed her, then beat and strangled her to death.

He claimed another victim on August 18, 1980, beating, strangling and robbing a 75-year-old man who he'd also previously known. Then, on November 11, he killed again, beating a 72-year-old woman to death with a wrench. The elderly victim also showed signs of sexual assault, with bruises and tears to the vaginal tissue. On December 6, Mason beat and strangled a 75-year-old woman to death. The victim was found with her clothes torn off and extensive cuts and bruises to her body.

In December 1980, Mason struck again, although this time he inexplicably let his victims live. After gaining entrance to a home under the pretense of selling firewood, Mason tied up the elderly residents and robbed them of $47,000 in coins and jewelry.

Mason was arrested in February 1981 and was found to be in possession of a sawn-off shotgun and a loaded pistol (later proved to have been used in the shooting death of his male lover).

But Mason wasn't done yet. Confined to the Alameda County Jail, he beat and strangled his cellmate to death on May 9, 1982. He then hung the victim from a shower rod in an attempt to make the murder look like suicide.

Mason soon confessed to his crimes and expressed a desire to be executed. This wish was granted to him on August 24, 1993, when having waived all further appeals, he went to the gas chamber at San Quentin.

David Maust

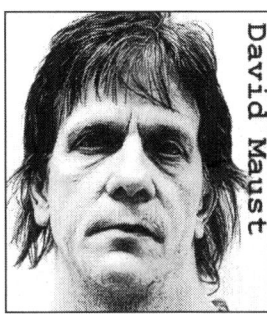

He was known as "Crazy Dave" in the neighborhood where he grew up, and with good reason too. David Maust's mother would later describe how, at age two, he would try to drop heavy objects onto his one-year-old sister's head; his brother would relate how a 7-year-old Dave once clubbed a squirrel to death with a baseball bat; the same brother narrowly escaped death when David tried to drown him. Undeterred, Maust later set fire to his brother's bed.

It was all too much for his mother to take and, at age 9, Maust was packed off to the Chicago State Hospital, a mental facility with a less than salubrious reputation. He remained there until 1967 when he was released to the Uhlich Children's Home. There, according to Maust's later testimony, he was sexually molested by another boy. He was returned to Chicago State in 1970 but escaped at age 17, never to return.

In 1971, at his mother's suggestion, Maust enlisted in the U.S. Army. In 1972, he was transferred to Germany and it was here that he committed his first murder. The victim was a 13-year-old boy, James McClister, who Maust had befriended. One day, for no apparent reason, he took the boy out to the woods, tied him to a tree and beat him to death with his fists and a wooden board.

McClister's body was found a month later and Maust was soon under arrest. Yet, because there were no witnesses to the murder, the charge was only manslaughter, and the sentence only 3 years at the military prison in Leavenworth, Kansas.

Released from that term, Maust returned to Chicago. In August 1981, he went looking for a teenage boy he had had sex with years before. Learning that the youth was now serving a jail term, Maust turned his attention to another boy, 15-year-old, Donald Jones. Having lured Jones into his car, Maust drove him to a quarry, where he stabbed the boy in the stomach before drowning him.

Maust fled to Texas but was soon in trouble after stabbing another teenager in a hotel room in Galveston. For that attack, he was sentenced to 5 years in a Texas jail.

In 1982, Maust was charged with the murder of Donald Jones, and in 1983 he was extradited from Texas to Illinois. His conviction in the Jones murder earned him a 35-year prison term, of which he served 17 years before being released in 1999.

Denied placement at a halfway house, Maust was reduced to living in homeless shelters and cheap hotels. In 2000, he moved to Oak

Park, Illinois, and in 2003 to Hammond, Indiana, where he obtained work at a shop that sold sports trophies.

Maust soon befriended a co-worker, Nick James, inviting the 19-year-old around to his house to drink and smoke marijuana. On May 3, 2003, Jones mysteriously disappeared.

Despite Maust's criminal past and his friendship with the young man, he was not suspected. Then, on September 10, 2003, two more Hammond teens, Michael Dennis, 13, and James Raganyi, 16, went missing. This time, Maust did come under suspicion and police obtained a search warrant for his rented house. They discovered freshly poured concrete in the basement and an evacuation yielded the bodies of the three missing teens.

Maust went on trial in 2005 and received three consecutive life terms without the possibility of parole. On January 20, 2006, he was found hanging in his cell, having fashioned a noose from a bed sheet. He died 27 hours later at St. Anthony Medical Center in Crown Point, Indiana.

Kenneth McDuff

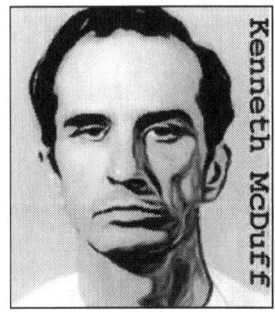

From an early age, it was evident to all who knew him that Kenneth McDuff was going to end up on the wrong side of the law. Born and raised in Texas, the hulking 6-foot-four teenager first attracted the attention of law enforcement officials while still in high school. Still, he managed to stay out of prison until 1965, when at age 19, he pulled a four-year term for a string of burglaries. Paroled after serving less than a year, McDuff responded by committing a brutal triple murder in Tarrant County.

On the night of August 6, 1966, McDuff and a buddy, Roy Dale Green, abducted three teenagers, Robert Brand, Mark Dunman, and Edna Louise Sullivan. After robbing their terrified victims, McDuff pushed Sullivan into the back seat of their car and forced the boys into the trunk. Driving the vehicle to an isolated spot, he threw open the trunk and shot Brand and Dunman to death as they begged for their lives. Then he and Green repeatedly raped Edna Sullivan before McDuff killed the girl by forcing a broomstick down on her throat.

McDuff was soon arrested for the murders and later convicted and sentenced to death. However, after the U.S. Supreme Court declared capital punishment unconstitutional in 1972, his sentence was reduced to life imprisonment.

Parole was not excluded and McDuff became eligible 1976, although subsequent parole boards wisely turned him down. Desperate, McDuff tried bribing a parole official in 1982 and saw two years added to his sentence.

McDuff remained in prison, but behind the scenes, things were working in his favor. As the inmate population in Texas soared and overcrowding became a serious problem, state officials tried to address the issue by paroling tens of thousands of inmates, many of them before they'd even served a single day inside.

Eventually, even a dangerous, cold-blooded killer like Kenneth McDuff, with 16 felony convictions, 12 burglaries and 3 murders to his name, warranted consideration. In October 1989, the unthinkable happened and McDuff was unleashed on an unwary public.

McDuff didn't stay out of trouble for long. By July 1990, he was back in prison after making a terrorist threat. Although this was reason enough to revoke his parole, prison officials again erred on the side of leniency and McDuff walked free on December 6, 1990.

Over the next 17 months, he unleashed a one-man crime wave on central Texas, a spree that is believed to have included as many as nine homicides.

McDuff would eventually be tried for two murders. On December 30, 1991, he abducted 28-year-old accountant, Colleen Reed, from an Austin car wash, raped, brutalized, and finally killed her. Then on March 1, 1992, he kidnapped, raped and killed Melissa Northrup, a pregnant, 22-year-old Waco convenience store clerk.

In the wake of the Northrup murder, McDuff became the subject of a massive manhunt. He escaped to Kansas City, Missouri, where he found work as a garbage collector. He was finally arrested on May 4, 1992, after he was featured on the TV show, America's Most Wanted.

By now, the death penalty had been reinstated in Texas (as in many other states) and there would be no escape for the brutal killer. Sentenced to death for the Reed and Northrup murders, he was executed by lethal injection on November 17, 1998. His final words (spoken to Warden Jim Willett) were: "I'm ready to be released. Release me."

The McDuff case triggered a massive overhaul of the Texas prison system. Parole rules were tightened and systems for monitoring potentially violent parolees were significantly strengthened. It addition extensive prison building projects were commissioned. These measures became known collectively as the "McDuff Laws."

David Meirhofer

David G. Meirhofer is not exactly a household name in the annals of crime, but he does occupy a unique position in American criminal history. Meirhofer was the first serial killer captured by the FBI using their groundbreaking offender profiling technique. Offender profiling seeks to uncover clues about an unknown offender from evidence left at the scene of a crime.

The crime that led to Meirhofer's eventual capture was the murder of seven-year-old Susan Jaeger. The little girl was snatched from her tent in the middle of the night during a family camping trip. At first, the disappearance was deemed to be a kidnapping, but when no ransom note arrived, investigators feared the worst. The FBI was called in and developed a profile that described the abductor as a young, white male who had taken the victim for sexual gratification and would likely kill her once she had served his purposes. They also believed that he might keep body parts of his victims as "souvenirs." Furthermore, they believed that he might have been arrested for other crimes.

This profile led them to a young man named David Meirhofer, 23 years old at the time. Meirhofer was already under suspicion for another murder, relating to the disappearance of his one-time girlfriend, Sandra Smallegan.

Brought in for questioning, Meirhofer denied any involvement in the disappearance of Susan Jaeger and as there was no physical evidence linking him to the crime, investigators were forced to let him go.

A year passed. Then, on the anniversary of Susan's disappearance, Meirhofer made a taunting call to her mother, Marietta Jaeger, boasting about what he'd done to her daughter. Marietta Jaeger was able to glean enough details from the call to lead FBI agents to Meirhofer.

Taken into custody, Meirhofer eventually broke down and confessed to killing Susan Jaeger and Sandra Smallegan. He also confessed to two more murders, those of Bernard Poelman, 13, and Michael Raney, 12.

Of the Smallegan murder, he said that he had decided to kidnap Sandra after she spurned his advances. They had dated once, he said, but thereafter she'd refused to see him. After overpowering Susan while she slept, he had tied her up and sealed her mouth with duct tape. However, he'd bound the tape too tightly and Smallegan had suffocated.

Meirhofer had then driven to the Lockhart ranch outside of Manhattan, Montana, where he'd dismembered Sandra's body and burned the remains in a fire.

On September 29, 1974, four hours after making his confession, Meirhofer tied a bath towel to his cell bars in the Gallatin County jail and hanged himself.

Frederick Mors

The case of Frederick Mors is one of the most peculiar in the annals of serial murder. Born Carl Menarik, in Vienna Austria, Mors immigrated to the United States in June 1914. He soon found employment at the German Old Fellows Home, a nursing home in the Bronx, New York City.

Mors was a strange person, who exhibited clear signs of megalomania. He traipsed around the wards dressed as a doctor, in a white coat, dangling a stethoscope from around his neck, and insisting that patients address him as "Herr Doktor." He ruled his ward with an iron fist, and his elderly charges were terrified of him. Everyone else, though, seems to have regarded him as eccentric, but harmless. Many seemed to enjoy his company and listened with interest to his fantastical tales about his exploits as a hunter.

Mors had not been working at the home long when an inordinately high number of patients started to die, 17 between September 1914 and January 1915 alone. Still, they were old and frail and in many cases their deaths appeared a mercy. Administrators at the home seemed content to let things be.

However, when it was learned that Mors had been buying large quantities of arsenic and chloroform from a local druggist, they realized that they must bring the matter to the attention of the police.

Mors beat them to it. On the afternoon of February 2, he arrived at a Bronx police station, dressed in a corduroy hunting outfit and a feathered alpine cap. Approaching the stunned desk sergeant, he confessed to the murders of eight "superannuated octogenarians." He'd killed them, he said, because they were a nuisance and he needed to "make room for more inmates" at the home.

A phone call to the care home confirmed the deaths and Mors was taken into custody, whereupon he swiftly changed his story. Now he said that the homicides had been ordered by officials at the home and that he was merely carrying out their instructions. The first victim had been killed with arsenic, he said, but when that had proven "troublesome" he'd switched to chloroform.

"First I would pour a drop or two of chloroform on a piece of absorbent cotton and hold it to the nostrils of the old person," he explained. "Soon my man would swoon. Then I would close the orifices of the body with cotton, stuffing it in the ears, nostrils and so on. Next, I would pour a little chloroform down the throat and prevent the fumes escaping the same way."

Based on Mors' testimony, the superintendent and three other employees of the home were arrested and held as material witnesses.

An exhumation of the remains would have cleared up the case, but the police refused to countenance it. Instead, they relied on witness testimony, and this seemed to confirm murder by chloroform. Mors had apparently warned one patient, Elizabeth Houser, of her impending death, and a mortician recalled seeing red marks - possibly chloroform burns - on the face of victim Henry Horn. A teenaged inmate told of delivering a bottle of chloroform to Mors from home employee Max Ring – one of those being held as a witness.

Yet, even with strong evidence of murder, Mors was never likely to be prosecuted. A psychiatric examination declared him "not mentally well" and he was committed to the Matteawan Institution for the Insane. His co-workers at the Old Fellows Home, meanwhile, were released, the case dismissed with a host of questions still unanswered.

On May 10, 1916, a week before his scheduled deportation to Austria, Mors escaped from custody and disappeared. He was never recaptured and his fate remains a mystery.

Gerald Parker

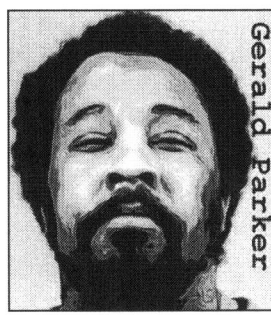

He was known as the "Bedroom Basher," a brutal, home-invading serial killer who terrorized Orange County in the 1970's. Over a period of two years, from 1978 to 79, Gerald Parker raped and bludgeoned five women to death in their homes near the El Toro Marine Corps Air Station, where he was serving as a U.S. Marine. He was also responsible for an attack on the wife of one of his fellow Marines, Kevin Lee Green, which resulted in the death of her near-full term fetus and led to Green being wrongfully imprisoned for 17 years.

Parker likely thought that he had gotten away with murder. But, in 1996, while revisiting the "Bedroom Basher" evidence, cold case investigators sent sperm retrieved from the victims for DNA analysis. They got an immediate hit to four victims - Kimberly Gaye Rawlins, 21, of Costa Mesa; Marilyn Kay Carleton, 31, of Costa Mesa; Debora Kennedy, 24, of Tustin; and Debra Lynn Senior, 17, of Costa Mesa. All were killed in 1979.

All samples were from the same man, a man currently serving time for the 1980 rape of a 13-year-old girl – Gerald Parker. With the DNA link established, Costa Mesa and Tustin detectives traveled to Avenal State Prison in Central California to interview Parker. He seemed almost relieved, as he confessed to each of the four murders as well as to a fifth, the rape / murder of 17-year-old Sandra Kay Fry in 1978. He then stunned investigators by admitting to the attack on Kevin Green's former wife, Dianna D'Aiello.

D'Aiello had been in the ninth month of her pregnancy at the time of the 1979 attack, which left her comatose for a month. Her injuries were so severe that doctors had to deliver the baby by cesarean section. The child was stillborn.

When Dianna regained consciousness, she told investigators that her husband, Kevin, had attacked her. He was promptly arrested and charged with murder and attempted murder. His alibi – that he was out buying a cheeseburger at the time of the attack – carried little weight with the jury. Despite passing a polygraph, he was sentenced to life imprisonment. A subsequent appeal was denied.

While incarcerated, Green steadfastly maintained his innocence and once DNA technology became available, he asked for the evidence to be re-examined. However, his request was turned down and as he lacked the money to pay for private testing, he remained in prison. Now, he was proved innocent, the real killer caught at last.

Gerald Parker went on trial in Orange County in January 1999. He was sentenced to die by lethal injection and currently awaits execution on California's death row at San Quentin.

Harry Powers

There can be few killers in the annals of American crime more depraved than Harry Powers. On the face of it, Powers (real name: Herman Drenth) was a respectable, married man, operating a grocery store with his wife in Clarksburg, West Virginia. Scratch below the surface, though, and an entirely different picture emerged, one of a deadly lothario who preyed on the lonely women he attracted through matrimonial bureaus like Detroit's American Friendship Society.

Powers' method was simple. He'd run an ad describing himself as a "Wealthy widower worth $150,000." He claimed to own a "beautiful 10-room brick home, completely furnished with everything that would make a good woman happy." "My wife would have her own car and plenty of spending money," he continued. "She would have nothing to do but enjoy herself."

A levelheaded assessment might suggest that these claims were simply too good to be true. And yet there were plenty of takers, including the woman whose death would eventually lead to Powers' downfall.

Asta Eicher was a 50-year-old Chicago widow with three children - Greta, 14; Harry, 12, and Anabel, 9. In July 1931, she told friends that she'd fallen in love with a Mr. Pierson, who she'd met through a matrimonial agency. At the same time, she asked her lodger William O'Boyle, to vacate the premises as Pierson was moving in.

In August, O'Boyle returned to the Eicher house to collect some tools he'd left behind. He found Mrs. Eicher and her children gone. But Pierson was there, and he was in the process of emptying the house. O'Boyle immediately informed the police.

Under questioning, Pierson said that the Eichers had moved to Colorado, and had asked him to settle their affairs. He even produced a letter to this effect, but as he could not provide details on the family's whereabouts, the police were suspicious. At the Eicher house, they found love letters that had passed between Pierson and Mrs. Eicher. Those led them to Quiet Dell, West Virginia, where Pierson lived under the name Harry Powers, with his wife, Luella.

Powers (Pierson) continued to insist that the Eichers had gone to Colorado, but he told conflicting stories and when the police searched his house they found jewelry and other items belonging to Mrs. Eicher. It was enough to obtain a search warrant for the property and on August 28, they unearthed the corpses of the widow and her three children. The following day another body, later identified as Dorothy Lemke, 50, of Northboro, Massachusetts, was uncovered. She'd been missing since July.

After a brutal interrogation by police, Powers confessed to the five murders, providing details that sickened even seasoned detectives. He said that he'd driven the Eichers from Chicago to his farm. There, he'd held them prisoner for a few days before leading them one by one to the garage where he'd hung them from the rafters. He'd forced 12-year-old Harry to watch the murders of his mother and sisters. When the boy started screaming, Powers bludgeoned him to death with a claw hammer.

No more bodies were found at the farm, but there was a strong suspicion that Powers had killed other victims, particularly as the police discovered a trunk-load of letters from more than 100 love-starved women from all over the country.

Asked how many he had killed, Powers simply shrugged his shoulders and muttered, "I don't know." Asked why he'd done it, he readily admitted deriving sexual pleasure from watching his victims' death throes. "It beat any cathouse I was ever in," he said.

Powers went to the gallows on March 18, 1932, taking with him to the grave the truth about how many women he'd murdered for pleasure and profit.

David Parker Ray

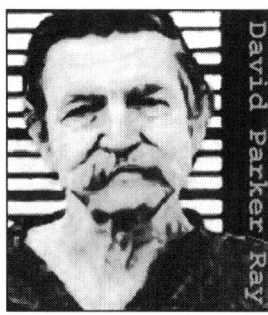

If the numbers are to be believed, David Parker Ray ranks among the most prolific serial killers in American history. Ray, along with several accomplices is suspected of as many as 60 murders, committed while he was living in the town of Truth Or Consequences, New Mexico.

The crimes were unique, both in their execution and the lack of bodies recovered from the site. David Parker Ray was far too clever for that. He abducted his prostitute victims from as far afield as Albuquerque and transported them to his personal torture chamber, his so-called "Toy Box" in the desert. This former mobile home had been converted at the cost of some $100,000. Inside, were a gynecologist's chair, whips, chains, pulleys, straps, clamps, leg spreader bars, surgical blades, and saws. In addition, Ray kept numerous sex toys, torture implements, syringes, and quantities of the drugs, sodium pentothal and phenobarbitol. There was video and audio recording equipment and a mirror placed above the chair, presumably so that victims could witness the atrocities being inflicted upon them. In addition, investigators found several hand-drawn diagrams showing various methods of inflicting pain.

Exactly how many women David Parker Ray dragged to his torture suite is unknown, but Ray was a meticulous planner and might have gotten away with his crimes indefinitely, had one of his victims not escaped.

On March 22, 1999, Cynthia Vigil was being held prisoner in the "Toy Box." Vigil had been kidnapped by Ray and his accomplice, Cindy Hendy, three days earlier. She had endured many hours of horrendous sexual torture by the pair and was weak from her injuries. Still, she realized that if she did not escape she was likely to be killed. Vigil waited until Ray went to work. Then, noticing that Hendy had carelessly left the handcuff keys on a table nearby, Vigil seized her chance.

While Hendy was talking on the phone in another room, Vigil managed to snag the keys and work herself loose. However, as she was about to make a run for it, Hendy reappeared. A fight ensued, during which Vigil was struck on the head with a lampshade. Clinging on to consciousness, she picked up an ice pick and stabbed Hendy in the neck before making her escape.

Naked, and with a metal slave collar still attached to her neck, Vigil ran to a neighboring trailer, about half a mile away. The owner then phoned the police and when Ray returned (having been summoned by Hendy) police officers were there to arrest him.

The evidence against Ray, including videotapes taken from the trailer, was overwhelming. Yet he still protested his innocence, insisting that he hadn't killed anyone and that the scenes of sexual torture depicted on the tapes were consensual.

Despite his protestations of innocence, Ray along with accomplices; Hendy, Ray's daughter, Glenda Jean "Jesse" Ray, and Dennis Yancy, were tried on various charges.

Yancy admitted to murdering a former girlfriend, Marie Parker, who had been kidnapped and tortured by Ray. He was convicted of second-degree murder and conspiracy to commit murder, and received two 15-year terms. Cindy Hendy received 36 years for her part in the crimes. Jesse Ray got nine years.

Ray, meanwhile, entered into a plea bargain and received 224 years in prison for numerous offenses relating to the abduction and sexual torture of three young women. He would serve none of that time.

On May 28, 2002, while being transported to the Lea County Correctional Facility in Hobbs, New Mexico, David Parker Ray died of a heart attack.

Efren Saldivar

Medical serial killers, doctors and nurses who prey on their patients, are notoriously difficult to detect. When they are caught, it is usually because colleagues or hospital administrators notice a spike in the number of deaths of patients under their care. Efren Saldivar was cleverer than that. He targeted the critically ill, those expected to die soon anyway, those with the notation "DNR" written on their medical charts – "Do Not Resuscitate." Convicted of six murders, Saldivar may have committed as many as 170, in a murderous career spanning from 1989 to 1997.

Born in Brownsville, Texas, on September 30, 1969, Saldivar moved to Los Angeles at an early age with his family. He attended school there and was a popular student, even though his grades were less than stellar. After flunking out in his senior year, he drifted through a number of menial jobs before seeing a friend in a medical uniform and deciding he wanted a medical career. In

1988, he took a high school equivalency test before enrolling at the College of Medical and Dental Careers in North Hollywood.

Saldivar graduated a year later, and immediately got a job as a respiratory therapist at Glendale Adventist Medical Center, working the night shift.

By all accounts, Saldivar was good at his job and his easy manner made him popular with patients. However, under his outgoing persona, Saldivar was suffering from depression, for which he was taking the drug, Zoloft. Still, that didn't affect his work performance and if people died on his shift, well, that was to be expected when dealing with the elderly and infirm. And Saldivar might have gotten away with it indefinitely, but for a series of coincidences in 1997.

First, another therapist, a man named Bob Baker, went to his supervisor and reported that he believed Saldivar was killing patients. Such rumors are not uncommon in hospitals, and as Baker was known to bear a grudge against Saldivar, the supervisor (who also disliked Saldivar) listened but explained that he was unable to act without evidence. The two men agreed to keep a close eye on Saldivar.

A while later, a few of Saldivar's colleagues decided to play a practical joke on him by putting someone else's clothes in his locker. However, they were in for a surprise when they forced the locker door. Inside they discovered a number of potent drugs, including morphine, succinylcholine chloride, and Pavulon, a drug used to stop the breathing of patients who were going onto a respirator. There were also a number of syringes, some of them used. Saldivar was not allowed to handle these drugs in his job, so their presence looked suspicious. However, because they'd been found while breaking into his locker, the nurses decided not to report it.

The incident that eventually brought the matter to police attention occurred when a nurse named Ursula Anderson told a man she'd met in a bar about the suspicions surrounding Saldivar. The man, Grant Brossus, saw an opportunity to make some money, and made a call to hospital administrators, suggesting that $50,000 might be an appropriate sum for his silence. Anderson hadn't given Saldivar's name to Brossus, but Glendale Adventist was concerned enough to call in the police.

The investigation eventually honed in on Saldivar and he was brought in for questioning. He was happy, he said, to have the opportunity to clear his name. However, he soon changed tack and admitted to injecting patients with Pavulon, the first not long after he'd started work at the hospital. Exhumations of several patients later found high concentrations of the drug in six of them and Saldivar was indicted for murder.

On March 12, 2002, he pleaded guilty to six counts and was sentenced to six consecutive life terms without the possibility of parole.

Altemio Sanchez

A brutal rapist and killer, Altemio Sanchez murdered at least three women and raped at least 14 more in a murderous career spanning 25 years from 1981 to 2006. His modus operandi of attacking his victims near secluded bicycle paths, earned him the nickname, the Bike Path Rapist.

Sanchez's first rape victim was a 44-year-old jogger who he rendered unconscious and then raped in Delaware Park, Buffalo, on June 12, 1986. Two days later, he attacked a 17-year-old student near Riverside High School and, over the next four years, he committed a series of rapes before escalating to murder on September 29, 1990.

Linda Yalem, a 22-year-old sophomore at the University of Buffalo was raped and strangled as she jogged near Ellicott Creek bicycle path. Her body was discovered a day later, concealed in thick undergrowth.

On October 30, 1992, Majane Mazur, a 30-year-old with a 5-year-old daughter, disappeared. Her body was discovered on November 22, in a field off Exchange Street in Buffalo. She'd been raped and strangled.

Two years later, on October 19, 1992, a 14-year-old high school student was raped at a junkyard in Riverside, Buffalo. The M.O. matched the other rapes and the police were certain that they had a serial rapist, and possibly a serial killer, on their hands. However, just when they appeared to be making progress in the case, the killer dropped out of sight. He would remain in the shadows for fourteen years.

On September 29, 2006, 45-year-old Joan Diver was attacked as she jogged near a bicycle path in Newstead, New York. Her body was discovered beside the path, raped, strangled and bludgeoned to death.

Fearing that the Bike Path Rapist might be back, the police decided to reinvestigate old clues. One of those dated to 1987. A rape victim had spotted a man she believed to be her attacker at a local mall. She followed him to the parking lot and jotted down his license plate number. The car turned out to belong to Wilfredo Caraballo, Sanchez's uncle.

At the time, Caraballo insisted that he hadn't taken the car out in months. But in January 2007, more than two decades later, he admitted that his nephew, Altemio Sanchez, had borrowed the car from him.

Armed with this information, the police placed Sanchez under surveillance and obtained a DNA sample off a glass he used in a restaurant. Within 24 hours, they had a match that told them Altemio Sanchez was the Bike Path Rapist.

Sanchez was arrested on January 15, 2007. On May 17, he pleaded guilty to three murders and a number of rape charges. On August 15, 2007, he was sentenced to 75 years in prison with no possibility of parole.

But the story doesn't end there. The arrest of Sanchez led to the release of Anthony Capozzi, who had served 22 years in prison for two rapes now definitely proven to have been committed by Sanchez. Neither are the police convinced that Sanchez has told them the whole truth. Senior police officers believe the true number of rapes he committed might be "incomprehensible."

Sanchez is also a suspect in the murder of a 15-year-old girl in 1985.

Altemio Sanchez is currently serving his time at Clinton State Prison, New York State's toughest correctional facility.

Heriberto Seda

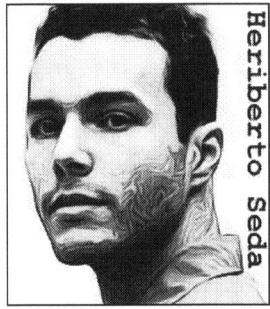

Imitation, so they say, is the surest form of flattery. Heriberto Seda certainly believed so, as he launched a campaign of terror against the citizens of New York City in deference to his hero, San Francisco's elusive "Zodiac Killer." Seda interpreted the infamous moniker more literally, though, he sent letters to the police boasting of a plot to kill victims based on their astrological symbols, one for each sign of the Zodiac.

At first, the police thought it was a hoax, but on March 8, 1990, they were proved horribly wrong when Soto shot Mario Orosco in the back and left him for dead. 21 days later, he attacked German Montenedro, who also survived. His next victim would not be so lucky. 71-year-old Joseph Proce was shot on May 31, 1990, he died in hospital three weeks later. A note found at the murder scene bore pictures of the Zodiac signs of the first three victims – Scorpio, Gemini, Taurus. Underneath was scrawled the message: "Zodiac – Time to die!"

The fourth victim, a homeless man named Larry Parham, was shot as he slept on a bench in Central Park on June 21. When he recovered from his wounds he told police that a man had approached him a few days before the shooting and asked him what his astrological sign was. A piece of paper bearing a picture of Parham's Zodiac sign was found near the crime scene. On that note, police found a fingerprint that would later nail the killer.

In the aftermath of the Parham shooting, "Zodiac" sent a number of letters to the media, before dropping out of sight. He reappeared on August 10, 1992, stabbing 39-year-old Patricia Fonte to death.

Ten months later, on June 4, 1993, Zodiac fired at James Weber, striking him in the leg; on July 20, he shot a 40-year-old homeless man, John DiAcone, to death; on October 2, he shot Diane Ballard in the neck, leaving her partially paralyzed.

It was not until a letter arrived at The New York Post in August of 1994 that these latest attacks were linked to the Zodiac shootings of 1990. Even so, investigators were uncertain whether the letters were written by the killer himself, or by some hoaxer. After his capture, saliva from the envelopes would prove that the letters had been sent by Heriberto Seda. But that was in the future, first, the police had to catch the killer.

The break in the case came on June 18, 1996, when Seda got into an argument with his half-sister, Gladys Reyes, and her boyfriend. During the argument, Seda pulled a gun and shot Gladys in the back as she ran for the front door. Seriously wounded, she made it to a neighbor's apartment and called the police.

A tense standoff ensued during which Seda fired several shots at police officers, before eventually surrendering. He was found to be in possession of 13 homemade zip guns, various pipe bombs, crossbows, and knives. Books found in his apartment included volumes on bomb making and on Satanism.

Seda was taken to the local police precinct, where he was asked to write a statement. While he was doing so, Sergeant Herbert, who had been involved in the hunt for the Zodiac killer, noticed that Seda's handwriting bore a striking similarity to the writing on the letters sent to the press. He decided to run a check on Seda's fingerprints and turned up a match to the note left in the 1990 Central Park attack.

Seda was tried and convicted of three murders in June 1998. He was sentenced to three life terms, and will likely never be released.

Anthony Allen Shore

Many homicide detectives have a case that they refuse to let go, a case that despite the lack of evidence, they remain determined to solve. For Houston PD detective Bob King that case was the murder of 9-year-old Diana Rebollar in August 1994. Diana disappeared on her way to the store to buy sugar for her mother to make lemonade. Her brutalized body was found the following day. She was wearing only a black Halloween T-shirt. A ligature was twisted tourniquet-style around her neck. She had been sexually assaulted.

The unique murder weapon linked the murder to another homicide. Maria del Carmen Del Estrada was a 21-year old illegal immigrant whose half-naked body had been found in the drive-through lane of a Dairy Queen restaurant on April 16, 1992. She'd been sexually assaulted and strangled to death.

Houston PD was certain that the same man was responsible for both murders, but with very little evidence to go on, the case soon went cold. Then, on July 6, 1995, 16-year-old Dana Sanchez disappeared while hitchhiking to her boyfriend's house.

Her body was found in a field at the end of North View Park on July 14, after an anonymous caller (believed to be the killer) phoned in its location to a local TV reporter. Once again the corpse bore the unique signature of the so-called "Tourniquet Killer," but although eyewitnesses reported seeing Dana getting into a cream-colored panel van, the trail led nowhere. The case remained unsolved for another eight years.

In October 2003, investigators sent genetic evidence from Maria Estrada's fingernails to Orchid Cellmark, a private forensic DNA laboratory in Dallas. On October 16, they got a match to Anthony Allen Shore, a tow truck driver whose DNA profile was on record due to a conviction for sexually molesting his own daughters.

Shore was taken into custody and subjected to intense interrogation, eventually confessing to the murders of Carmen Del Estrada, Diana Rebollar, and Dana Sanchez. He also admitted to the 1987 murder of 14-year old Laurie Tremblay and the 1994 rape of another 14-year-old girl. Tremblay had been on her way to school when she was abducted and killed, her body dumped behind a Mexican restaurant.

The police did not initially link her murder to the other three because she was not sexually assaulted and was strangled with a ligature rather than a tourniquet. When asked why he switched to using the tourniquet Shore replied: "Because I hurt my finger while murdering Tremblay."

Anthony Shore went on trial in October 2004. Despite his confession to four murders, prosecutor Kelly Siegler decided to charge him only with the Estrada homicide, since the DNA evidence made it the strongest case. Evidence of the other three murders and the rape was however introduced in the punishment phase and the outcome was always a forgone conclusion. Shore asked for the death penalty and the jury was happy to oblige, taking just an hour to return their recommendation.

Anthony Allen Shore currently awaits execution on death row at Livingston, Texas. Investigating officers firmly believe that he has committed more than the four murders he confessed to. He remains a prime suspect in a series of homicides committed along I-45, bearing his unique signature.

Daniel Siebert

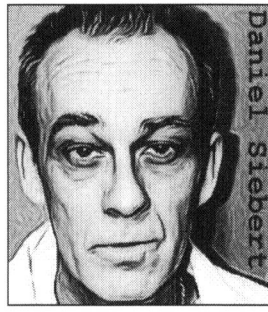

On February 24, 1986, a counselor at the Alabama Institute for the Deaf and Blind, in Talladega, placed a call to the manager of a nearby apartment complex. He was concerned about one of his students, hearing-impaired Sherri Weathers, who had not been to class in the previous week. The apartment manager invited the counselor to call on the building and the two men then went to Weathers' apartment, which they entered using a passkey. They found Sherri inside, lying on the bed with her sons, Chad, 5, and Joseph, just 4-years-old. All three had been strangled.

After the police arrived and began their inquiries, they learned of another student, 33-year-old Linda Jarman, who was recently missing from the Institute. Jarman lived in the same building, and a search of her apartment turned up her nude, strangled body. Her killer had also stolen her television set and her car.

Continuing their investigation at the Institute, the police found out that one of the faculty, an art teacher named Daniel Spence, had expressed a romantic interest in Sherri Weathers. Not much was known about Spence. He'd apparently shown up at the school several months earlier, offering to teach for free in the hope of gaining a position. More tellingly, he had not been seen since February 20.

He had, however, left his fingerprints behind at the Talladega murder scenes. They identified him as Daniel Siebert, convicted of manslaughter in Las Vegas in 1979, and currently wanted in San Francisco for assault.

Siebert had recently been dating a 32-year-old cocktail waitress named Linda Odum, but Linda was unable to assist them with their inquiries. She'd been reported missing on February 24, and now Siebert was missing too, apparently on the run.

On March 3, 1986, Highway patrol officers found Linda Odum's car abandoned near Elizabethtown, Kentucky. Siebert's fingerprints were lifted from the vehicle. Then on March 30, Odum's naked, decomposed corpse was found outside of Talladega. Siebert was now wanted for five murders and a sixth charge followed after he was connected via forensic evidence to the murder of a prostitute in

Calhoun County.

Over the next six months, sightings of the elusive Siebert were reported from Ohio, New Jersey, Nevada, California, and Canada. Then, on September 3, 1986, Siebert made the fatal mistake of calling a friend in Las Vegas. The friend reported the call to police and when Siebert called again they ran a trace and tracked him to Memphis, Tennessee. Siebert was arrested the next day, as he showed up for work.

In custody, Siebert quickly confessed to the murders in Alabama plus various others across America. When he was asked how many, he answered nonchalantly: "Maybe a dozen, maybe more. I try to put those things out of my mind." He killed for purposes of sex and robbery, being careful to murder his victims after a San Francisco hooker survived a throttling and filed charges against him.

Aside from the Alabama cases, Siebert would eventually be tried for three murders, while he is also a suspect in unsolved homicides in Arizona, California, Nevada and Florida.

On March 21, 1987, he was sentenced to death in Alabama, but it was a sentence that would never be carried out. Siebert died of cancer on April 22, 2008, after serving more than 21 years on death row.

Jack Spillman III

In April 1995, a young woman called on the East Wenatchee, Washington, home of her mother, Rita Huffman. She'd been unable to raise a reply on the phone from her mother or 14-year-old sister, Amanda, and she was worried about them. The front door was locked, so she went around to a rear door that she knew was always left unlocked.

As she stepped into the home, she immediately sensed that something was wrong. Then her worse fears were realized when she discovered the bodies of her mother and sister, so drenched in blood that it appeared they'd been torn apart by a wild animal. She bolted from the house and ran to a neighbor who called the police.

Officers responding to the call, found a scene that turned their stomachs. Amanda lay on the bed in her mother's bedroom. She'd been stabbed and bludgeoned, then raped, after which her killer had forced a baseball bat into her vagina. He'd also disemboweled her, and placed skin from her genitals onto her face. A stopped watch on her wrist suggested that death had occurred around 11:35.

Rita was left lying on a couch in the family room. Her body bore 31 stab wounds and she'd been savagely mutilated, her breasts cut off and placed in the bedroom next to Amanda. Her vagina had been cut out and shoved into her mouth, and she'd been explicitly posed.

The brutal nature of the murders terrified investigators. Someone who killed with such obvious savagery would definitely kill again unless they caught him quickly.

Fortunately, the murderer they sought was a less than competent criminal. Checking incident reports for the night of the murders, detectives found that a man dressed all in black had been arrested not far from the crime scene at 2 a.m. that morning, on suspicion of burglary. Officers went back to the location where he'd been apprehended and found a bloody knife. They also found a witness who'd seen the man's truck parked near the crime scene at around 11:30.

The man's name was Owen Spillman III, and he had since been released from custody. He was immediately placed under surveillance while investigators looked into his background. What they found strengthened their belief that Spillman was their man. He had a record for rape and burglary and was suspected in the disappearance of a 9-year-old girl, the daughter of a woman he'd been living with.

While under surveillance, Spillman disposed of a blood-soaked ski mask, which detectives recovered and sent for testing. It provided a match to the victims (as did the knife the police had recovered earlier). A bloodstain near the mouth opening of the mask suggested that Spillman had pressed his mouth to a wound. (He'd later admit to drinking Amanda's blood).

The police now had enough to arrest Spillman and obtain a search warrant for his car and residence. These added a wealth of forensic evidence in the form of blood, hair, and fibers. It was also learned that Spillman was employed as a butcher, which explained the precise cuts to the bodies.

Faced with the almost certain prospect of the death penalty, Spillman struck a bargain, exchanging a confession for life in prison. He also admitted to killing Penny Davis, the 9-year-old daughter of his former lover, and led investigators to where he'd buried her body.

While being held pending trial, Spillman reportedly told his cellmate that he thought of himself as a werewolf and wanted to become "the most famous serial killer in the country." He said that he'd studied other killers to learn their techniques. He also admitted that after killing and burying Penny Davis, he'd exhumed her body several times for sexual purposes.

Spillman was sentenced to life in prison without the possibility of parole, to be served at Washington's tough Walla Walla prison.

James Swann

For two bloody months in early 1993, a serial shooter terrorized the Mount Pleasant and Columbia Heights neighborhoods of Washington D.C. The "Shotgun Stalker," chose his targets entirely at random, firing at them from a slow moving vehicle. By the time he was done, four victims, two male and two female, lay dead, while several others had suffered serious injuries.

The first attack occurred on February 23, 1993, when the shooter fired at a woman walking along Monroe Street - and missed. The woman reported the incident but the police wrote it off as a prank, saying the weapon was most likely an air rifle. Yet even as officers were dismissing the attack, another victim was shot. The 22-year-old male was seriously injured, losing an eye and the use of one arm as a result.

On March 4, two weeks after the first two shootings, the shooter returned, firing at a pedestrian and striking him in the head. The 43-year-old man survived but suffered severe injuries. The police put it down to gang-related warfare.

There was no disguising the next attack, though. This one took place in upscale Mount Pleasant and the female victim had no connection to gangs or the drug trade. Still, her wounds were superficial, so police hypothesized that she was just an innocent bystander.

As if to answer that speculation, the killer showed up again in Mount Pleasant on March 23. The victim was 28-year-old Elizabeth "Bessie" Hutson, shot and killed as she walked her dogs. Now, at last, the police sat up and took notice. It appeared there was a serial shooter loose on the streets of the nation's capital. And judging by the rate of his attacks, he'd be back soon.

That prediction proved accurate on April 4, when the stalker fired at a woman walking on Holmead Place. On April 10, he returned to Holmead Place, firing at three pedestrians, killing one, a 35-year-old man.

On April 19, he launched his boldest attack yet, taking shots at three pedestrians in Columbia Heights in broad daylight, despite the presence of increased police patrols. One of those victims, a 61-year-old woman shot on 13th Street, died. The shooter's death toll was now four.

However, as he fled the scene, police caught a lucky break. Kenneth Stewart, an off-duty police officer, spotted a blue Toyota running a red light on Sherman Avenue and gave chase. He eventually trapped the vehicle in the parking lot of a plumbing supplies store and took the driver into custody. The man, James Swann, had a recently fired shotgun lying on the back seat that tied him to the shooting spree. After a total of 14 attacks and four homicides, the nightmare was finally over. Now began the process of bringing the deadly shooter to justice.

That task was easier said than done. It did not take long for investigators to realize that their suspect wasn't shuffling from a full deck. Unlike most serial killers, who stick to hunting grounds that they're familiar with, Swann was actually driving from New Jersey to D.C. to commit his violence. The reason was simple he said, the evil spirit of Malcolm X had commanded him to shoot people in Northwest Washington.

Why these neighborhoods, in particular, he was asked. Because, Swann explained, the people of northwest D.C. were responsible for the 1965 assassination of Malcolm X in New York.

Unsurprisingly, Swann was declared "not guilty by reason of insanity." He was committed to Saint Elizabeth's, a mental hospital, and remains confined to this day.

John Floyd Thomas, Jr.

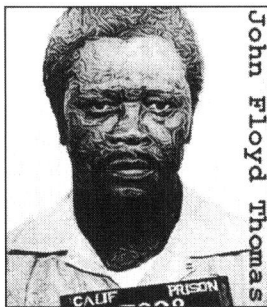

Although the stereotypical serial killer profile describes a white male in his mid-twenties or early thirties, serial killers come in all hues, ages and genders. Black serial killers are by no means a rarity. In fact, proportional to the population, they are slightly more prevalent than their Caucasian counterparts. Another statistic indicates that a disproportionate percentage of serial killers who target the elderly are black – Carlton Gary, Howard Arthur Allen, and the British serial strangler, Kenneth Erskine, among them. Another example is John Floyd Thomas Jr.

The murders attributed to Thomas occurred in two distinct waves, the first of which was spread across a swathe of Los Angeles - from Hollywood to Inglewood - in the 1970's. At least 17 elderly women fell victim to an unknown assailant dubbed the "Westside Rapist" by police. The killer entered his victims' homes, raped and then choked them to death. Typically, the bodies were found with pillows or blankets placed over their faces.

The killings reached their zenith in 1978, then suddenly stopped. This coincided with Thomas's arrest and incarceration on an unrelated rape charge.

Thomas was released in 1983. Not long after, the murders started up again, this time in Claremont, California, 40 miles east of Los Angeles. In quick succession, five elderly women were raped and strangled in their homes, their faces left covered by the killer. Then, as abruptly as they'd started, the murders stopped, coinciding with Thomas moving from the area to take a job in Glendale.

Despite the obvious similarities in the killer's M.O., the police did not link the two waves of killings because survivors of the attacks gave differing descriptions of the assailant. The case was left languishing until the Los Angeles Police Department established a Cold Case Homicide Unit in 2001. Then, the case was one of those selected for re-evaluation using newly available DNA techniques.

In 2004, the crime lab matched DNA taken from two of the victims to a single perpetrator, but could not find a suspect in the state's embryonic DNA database.

However, moves were already afoot to expand that database by incorporating DNA from convicted sex offenders. It was a mammoth undertaking and it was five years before Thomas was required to provide a swab (pursuant to his 1978 rape conviction). Once his sample was entered into the system, investigators had their hit, tying him not only to the Claremont murders, but to the "Westside Rapist" slayings of the 1970's as well.

Thomas was arrested on March 31, 2009. On April 2, he was charged with the murders of Ethel Sokoloff in November 1972 and Elizabeth McKeown in February 1976. On September 23, five further murder charges were added, those of Cora Perry in September 1975; Maybelle Hudson in April 1976; Miriam McKinley in June 1976; Evalyn Bunner in October 1976, and Adrian Askew in June 1986.

Thomas is currently being held without bail at the LA County Jail. If found guilty of the crimes of which he is accused, he is likely to face the death penalty.

Chester Turner

Los Angeles, California has produced its fair share of serial killers. Many, like "Night Stalker" Richard Ramirez, "Freeway Killer" William Bonin, and "Sunset Slayer" Douglas Clark have achieved lasting infamy. Yet one of the city's most prolific killers is unknown to all but the most dedicated true crime buffs.

In 1987, South Los Angeles cops began to suspect that a serial killer was at work along the Figueroa Corridor, a 30-block stretch known mainly for drugs and prostitution. Starting in May of that year, the bodies of African-American prostitutes started showing up, dumped in parks, alleys, along roadsides, even in a local schoolyard.

The LAPD responded by establishing a Task Force and within a short time had questioned dozens of suspects. Yet the killer in their midst, a local man renowned for his fiery temper, never attracted their attention.

This is understandable. Chester Turner blended in perfectly with his environment. A high school dropout who still lived at home with his mother, Turner had had a couple of minor brushes with the law. But there was nothing to suggest the 11-year reign of terror he would unleash.

The first murder occurred when Turner was 20-years-old and working as a deliveryman for Domino's Pizza. Diane Johnson, 21, was found partially nude in a roadway construction area west of the Harbor Freeway in May 1987. A short while after, Elandra Bunn was found near 98th and Figueroa streets. Then Annette Ernest's nude body was found, just three blocks from where Johnson was discovered. All three women had been raped.

The killings stopped for a while after that (it later turned out that Turner had been shot during an argument with a relative of his girlfriend), but they resumed in early 1989, when Anita Fishman, 31, disappeared. Her badly decomposed body was found two weeks later, hidden under a mattress in an alley.

Nine months later, Regina Washington, six-and-a-half months pregnant, was found hanging by an electrical cord inside a garage. Still, the police had nothing to suggest Turner as a suspect. He was by this time training to be a manager at Domino's. When he did acquire another arrest, it was for lewd conduct, masturbating in public.

Turner pulled jail time for that offense, but he was out again in September 1992. Three weeks after his release, the body of

Tammie Christmas was found at Barrett Elementary School on West 98th Street. Debra Williams was discovered in a stairwell at the same school on November 16, and a month later Mary Edwards was found at a rundown hotel next to the school. All of these sites were within easy walking distance of Turner's home.

Andrea Tripplett vanished on April 2, 1993, after being seen getting into a car with an African-American man. Just over a month later, in May 1993, the body of Desarae Jones was found in a backyard.

In 1994, Turner left Los Angeles and moved to Salt Lake City, where his mother now lived. There, he worked at a homeless shelter but returned to L.A. in early 1995. Soon after, the body count resumed, with the February 1995 murder of 31-year-old Natalie Price.

In November 1996, the partially nude body of 45-year-old Mildred Beasley was found hidden in bushes beside the 110 Freeway. Beasley had only recently moved to L.A. from Texas. She was Turner's last victim in South L.A. before he shifted his killing ground downtown.

In early 1998, Turner was living at a downtown hotel when he lured a transient named Paula Vance to a footpath next to an office building. There a security camera captured Vance's brutal rape and murder, but unfortunately did not show the face of her killer.

Two months later, Brenda Bries was found strangled to death in a portable toilet, sited just 50 yards away from the Regal Hotel, where Turner was staying at the time.

Turner's next victim was known to him but for some reason, Turner did not kill Maria Martinez after he raped her. Instead, he warned her not to report the incident and released her.

Fortunately, Martinez wasn't cowed. She went directly to the police and Turner soon found himself under arrest. With a suspect in custody, DNA testing did the rest, linking Turner forensically to 13 murders.

Turner was tried and convicted for the murders of ten women, plus the unborn child of Regina Washington. He currently awaits execution on Death Row at San Quentin.

Faryion Wardrip

Over a period of 18 months, from December 1984 to May 1986, the citizens of Wichita Falls, Texas, lived in terror of a vicious serial killer. The murderer first struck on December 20, 1984, brutally slaying 20-year-old Terry Lee Sims, a Midwestern State University education major. Sims was found in the bathroom at a friend's home. Her hands were tied with an electrical cord and she'd been stabbed 11 times. She'd also been raped.

Less than two months later, on February 15, 1985, the brutalized body of 24-year-old nurse, Toni Jean Gibbs, was found in a field in Archer County. Like the previous victim, she'd been raped and then repeatedly stabbed.

A third victim turned up on March 29, when the body of 25-year-old Debra Taylor was found in a field in Fort Worth. Taylor had sustained blunt-force trauma to her head and face but had been killed by manual strangulation. The medical examiner was unable to determine whether or not she had been sexually assaulted.

On October 10, 1985, a county maintenance crew, working along a stretch of road in Wichita County, found the decomposed corpse of Ellen Blau. The state of decomposition was such that the coroner could not determine cause of death, although it was clear that she'd been murdered.

Six months later, on May 6, 1986, the body of 22-year-old Tina Elizabeth Kimbrew was found on the floor of her ransacked apartment in Wichita Falls. Kimbrew had numerous bruises on her face, neck, and legs. Her nightgown was pulled up and her underwear was on the floor near her body. However, there was no evidence of recent sexual activity. The doctor who performed the autopsy concluded that Kimbrew had been smothered to death.

With the city now in an uproar and terrified citizens stocking up on guns and ammunition, the police needed a quick arrest, and they got one when 26-year-old Faryion Edward Wardrip was brought in for questioning and promptly admitted to killing Tina Kimbrew. However, he denied involvement in the other murders, and with no physical evidence or eyewitness testimony, the police were forced to let the matter drop.

Wardrip pled guilty to the murder of Tina Kimbrew at his 1986 trial and was sentenced to 35 years in prison. He was released on parole in 1997, at which time the other murders remained unsolved.

And so it would likely have remained. Wardrip got on with his life, married and became a regular churchgoer. He even took to teaching Sunday school at the Church of Christ in his hometown of Olney.

Then, in 1999, cold case detectives sent sperm recovered from the Sims and Gibbs cases for DNA analysis. They got a hit to Faryion Wardrip.

Wardrip was arrested at his place of work in February 1999. He confessed to the Simms and Gibbs murders and also to those of Debra Taylor and Ellen Blau. He remains a suspect in several other homicides committed in the area in the period that he was active.

Wardrip was sentenced to death on November 9, 1999. That sentence was subsequently overturned and he was given life in prison without the possibility of parole.

Karl Warner

On August 3, 1969, school friends Deborah Furlong, 14, and Kathy Snoozy, 15, decided to cycle to a wooded hill overlooking their homes in the rugged Alameda Valley area of South San Jose, California. Packing a picnic lunch, the girls set off on their bicycles expecting to spend a pleasant afternoon in each other's company. What they found instead was an agonizing death at the hands of a vicious psychopath.

When the girls had not returned by early evening, Deborah Furlong's father went looking for them. He'd barely started up the hill when he came across a crowd of onlookers, being held back by police tape. Pushing to the fore, he witnessed a sight that no parent should ever see, his daughter and her friend lying on the ground, their bloodied, severely mutilated bodies among a grove of trees, within sight of their homes.

The medical examiner would record over 300 stab wounds to each victim, all of them inflicted above the waist. So severe were the injuries that the M.E. would later tell the press: "The Nazi sex mutilations during World War II were nothing compared to what was done to these young girls."

The murders threw the quiet Alameda Valley community into a state of shock and angry parents responded by launching street patrols, stopping and questioning any stranger found in the area. Little did they know that the killer was one of their own.

Homicide investigators, meanwhile, were under intense pressure to make an arrest, no easy task when all they had were wild theories foisted upon them by concerned members of the public.

One popular hypothesis was that an offshoot of the Manson family had committed the murders; another held that the elusive "Zodiac," an unidentified serial killer active in San Francisco at the time, was responsible. These speculations were wildly off the mark and the killer would remain at large for nearly two more years. Unfortunately, it would take another brutal slaying before he was eventually captured.

On April 11, 1971, 18-year-old Kathy Bilek walked the same hill where Debby Furlong and Kathy Snoozy had died nearly two years earlier. She had planned on bird watching. Instead, a serial killer found her. Kathy was stabbed 17 times in the back, 32 times in the chest and stomach, her body left on the hillside to be discovered the following morning. Given the nature of her injuries, investigators were sure that the same man was responsible and redoubled their efforts to catch him.

The break they'd been waiting for came two weeks later when a suspicious man, later identified as Karl F. Warner, was spotted walking in the area. Background checks revealed that Warner was a college student, but that he'd previously attended Oak Grove High School, the same school as the first two victims, Furlong and Snoozy. He lived with his parents just three blocks from the homes of the murdered girls and was currently a suspect in the stabbing of a woman who had survived her wounds.

Police secured a warrant and surprised Warner as he prepared for a college physics test. Their search turned up the murder weapon and Warner was taken into custody. He entered guilty pleas to all charges in September 1971 and was sentenced to life imprisonment.

John Francis Wille

On 6 June 1985, police officers in Laplace, Louisiana, some 40 miles from New Orleans, received a missing person report on an 8-year-old girl named Nichole Lapatta. Officers quickly arranged a search, which spread out from the Lapatta residence into nearby woods. There, near a makeshift garbage dump, they discovered the battered body of the missing child. She'd been brutally raped and strangled.

Close by, officers discovered another corpse, this one floating in the polluted waters of a canal. He was later identified as 25-year-old Billy Phillips, of Tickfaw, Louisiana. Phillips had been stabbed at least 84 times in a frenzied attack. In addition, his hands had been cut off and his genitals severely mutilated.

About a month after the gruesome discoveries, 26-year-old Frank Powe was hitchhiking near Bagdad, Florida, when a state trooper pulled over and warned him to get off the highway. Powe, unfortunately, didn't heed the warning. Later that day, his battered corpse was discovered by the roadside, the victim of an apparent hit-and-run.

That same day, Sheriff's deputies in Milton, Florida, were called to attend to a domestic disturbance. 21-year-old John Wille and his girlfriend were weeks behind on their rent and their landlord demanded that they vacate the premises. Wille refused and threatened violence, but backed down and left when the police arrived. However, he snuck back later and set fire to the landlord's mobile home.

Arrested and charged with first-degree arson, Wille denied setting the fire. However, his girlfriend was not so discreet, sharing with police officers details of a horrific murder spree spanning four states.

According to her story, Wille had committed a number of random and mostly unprovoked murders, including that of Frank Powe. She said that Wille had picked Powe up outside Bagdad but had become enraged when Powe had begun flirting with her. Beating the young man unconscious, Wille had dumped him in the bed of the pickup, then driven for several miles before unloading him on the road surface and deliberately driving over him.

Wille had also set the Milton trailer fire, the woman said, and was also responsible for another arson, years earlier in which a woman had died.

Following up on this lead, Florida law officers contacted their counterparts in

LaPlace, Louisiana, and confirmed the 1980 arson death of 78-year-old Ida Bodreaux. With the LaPlace connection established, Wille was soon linked forensically to the deaths of Nichole Lapatta and Billy Phillips.

Wille was also suspected of killing a Houston motorist, and of abducting and murdering Pensacola cab driver, Michael Foulk, whose body was found dumped in a ditch near Fairhope, Alabama.

Faced with the mounting evidence against him, Wille broke down and confessed to five murders. He later recanted his confessions but pled guilty to killing Frank Powe as part of a plea agreement.

That saved him from the death penalty in Florida, but Wille still had to face trial in Louisiana for the Lapatta and Phillips murders. This time, there would be no reprieve. He was sentenced to die in the electric chair.

For more True Crime books by Robert Keller please visit

http://bit.ly/kellerbooks

Printed in Great Britain
by Amazon